Swell to Great

Swell to Great

A Backward Look
from My Organ Loft

———◆———

Roberta Bitgood

with
Julia Goodfellow

———◆———

THE BAYBERRY DESIGN COMPANY, LLC
SALEM, CONNECTICUT, USA

2000

All illustrations are from Roberta Bitgood's private collection
unless otherwise noted.

"My Teacher" by Arliss Benham
© 1981 American Guild of Organists. Reprinted by permission.

Printed and bound in the United States of America
The paper used in this publication meets the minimum
requirements of the American National Standard for Permanence
of Paper for Printed Library Materials Z39-48-1984.

Cover illustrations:
front—At the Moller console of Holy Trinity Lutheran Church,
Buffalo, New York, ca. 1950;
back—At home, 1999, photo by Julia Goodfellow

Cover and book design by
The Bayberry Design Company, LLC

Published by
The Bayberry Design Company, LLC
Salem, Connecticut, U.S.A. 06420-3800
http://www.bayberrydesign.com

Library of Congress Card Number: 00-106981

ISBN 0-9673239-1-6

CONTENTS

———

Foreword by Rev. Dr. John C. B. Webster . vii
Introduction by Julia Goodfellow ix

A Backward Look

1   Surprise Election 3
2   Music Lessons 7
3   Family Portrait 13
4   Best View 21
5   Connecticut College 28
6   Wheels 32
7   Graduate Work 35
8   Bloomfield 45
9   Bert 57
10 Grace 64
11 Buffalo 72
12 Riverside 78
13 From California to Michigan 81
14 Detroit, Bay City, and Battle Creek . 84
15 Compositions 88
16 Teaching 96
17 Retirement 102

Reminiscences by Friends & Colleagues

18 Bloomfield 119
19 Buffalo 124
20 Riverside 134
21 Michigan 144
22 Best View 177

Antiphonal by Grace Wiersma 199

Appendix A: *Published Works
                of Roberta Bitgood* 202

Appendix B: *The Roberta Bitgood Archive
                at Connecticut College* 205

Index of Names 207

FOREWORD

John C. B. Webster

When I began as pastor of the Waterford United Presbyterian Church in September 1984, I discovered that our volunteer organist was leaving on a trip with her husband, who had just retired, and that she wanted me to find a permanent replacement for her, as they planned to do more travelling. In the meantime, she had arranged for Roberta Bitgood to fill in while she was away.

After one Sunday of hearing Roberta play, the chair of the personnel committee and I asked if she would be interested in making the arrangement permanent. The meeting was a bit awkward and Roberta was noncommittal, so I arranged a private visit with her. We already had Union Theological Seminary in common, so I shared with her my own very classical musical background as well as my views about the role of music in the life of the church. We were compatible and have remained so!

In that way, Roberta became this relatively new congregation's first professional organist, choir director, and director of music. Those who know her will not be surprised to learn that she was far more flexible about salary than about following AGO guidelines in her contract.

Roberta and I worked together for close to ten years. Our church worshipped in Harkness Chapel at Connecticut College when we began. In September 1989, we moved into our own building and renamed the church Crossroads Presbyterian Church. Roberta had given us valuable input on how to make the acoustics as good as possible and put us in touch with Alan McNeely, who built the pipe organ right into the sanctuary as the church was nearing completion. Alan gave us an unbelievably affordable price on that organ—now named for Roberta—in part because he could work on it with her. When the new church opened, the organ was ready and the choir sang a new anthem which Roberta had composed for the occasion.

The music during those ten years was memorable. Roberta brought out the best in the choir, no matter how many or how few were present, and we must have heard every one of Roberta's own compositions. My favorite will always be her cantata *Job* because I joined the choir for that one and thus got to know it best. She always arranged excellent music for our Christmas Eve services and preceded the 11 p.m. service with a half-hour organ recital, which set a special mood for the lessons and carols.

For me personally, the music that meant the most were the hymns, Sunday after Sunday. Roberta knows how to play hymns the way they should be played, and so the congregation could sing them the way they should be sung. Playing them right was not just a matter of getting the notes, stops, pedals, rhythm and volume right; it went deeper than technique. Roberta seemed to get inside each hymn, old or new, so that her accompaniment enabled us to both experience and express its particular power in the singing of it.

Roberta's gift goes beyond skill or talent, impressive and indispensable as those were; it is a gift of the Spirit as well, nurtured over decades of playing in church services. It is as though she had internalized those hymns; they became a part of her, part of her own spirituality, so that they might become part of us and our spirituality as well. That I dare say, when all is said and done, has been her greatest gift to us.

Christianity is a corporate faith and we who are "up front" and "performing" render our greatest service when we enable everyone else to get caught up in it, at its heights and in its depths. This Roberta did regularly at the organ, week in and week out, and I shall always be grateful.

May 3, 2000
Waterford, Connecticut

INTRODUCTION

Julia Goodfellow

It is hard to remember exactly when the idea came to me to help Roberta document her amazing life story, but it was probably around the time of the Bitgood Jubilee held on her 85th birthday, in 1993. It started with a strong suggestion to Roberta and Grace Wiersma, her daughter, and by the summer of 1997, while attending the New England regional convention of the AGO with Roberta, I became determined to launch this project in earnest.

Gathering the stories recounted in this book has involved a number of very enjoyable visits to Quaker Hill, Connecticut, to quiz Roberta and record her memories. Agnes Armstrong, who had previously interviewed Roberta for *The American Organist*, was gracious in permitting me to use some material from her articles, enabling me to avoid unnecessary duplication of effort.

It was in January 2000 that I finished my sweep of the available information. It became apparent then that there were gaps that still needed to be filled. In Roberta's own words, at age 92, her mind was beginning to be "somewhat like a sieve." So the idea emerged to solicit the recollections of various people who have known and loved Roberta. The AGO national headquarters was willing to support this effort by printing a small notice in its magazine soliciting personal recollections for a Bitgood biography.

The outpouring of stories and tributes has been overwhelming. I am convinced, moreover, that it could have continued for years. At some point, however, it seemed more important to have a finished project than a comprehensive one, and so with some regret about the contributions still in progress, we decided there had to be a cutoff date.

While relating some of these anecdotes to Roberta over the phone, I've heard her chuckle: "I don't remember that, but I'm willing to take so-and-so's word that it happened."

For the last few months, the furniture and floor in my family room have been covered with stacks of papers and letters. My husband Bill and daughter Ann have been most tolerant while other things have had to be put on hold. I feel fortunate to have had the support of my grown daughters, Marsha, Laura, and Alisa, who grew up knowing and loving Roberta, and who are now all involved in church music. Credit goes to my parents, Martha and Adrian Hoopengardner, who saw to it that I had music lessons, without which I never would have met Roberta, and to my aunt, Wilda Hoopengardner Reid, whose autobiography gave me a model for this book.

Grace Wiersma undertook the enormous task of selecting the photos to be included in the book, and she and her husband, Stuart, have been the capable business leaders of the venture. They have facilitated negotiations with Bill and Mary Anne Stewart of The Bayberry Design Company, LLC, whose elegant production of a similar book was inspiration for me to keep going with the project.

The manuscript itself would never have come into being if it hadn't been for Colleen Pace, who agreed to type it into a computer. I pulled Colleen out of retirement as an academic secretary at the University of Michigan–Flint, where she had previously typed numerous master's theses, doctoral dissertations, and university-level textbooks. During many an odd hour, we sat holed up in her basement office sorting through the myriad incidents in the life of this incredible woman. Colleen has an amazing capacity to decipher even the most complicated of manuscripts, and she has persevered through many revisions.

It is with much joy that *the project* is finally being sent off to the printer in order that the amazing story of Roberta's life can be preserved for future generations of church musicians. It is hoped that this book will serve as a memento for her many fans and friends, and most importantly as a sentimental journey and affirmation for Roberta of the outstanding impact and influence she has been and continues to be.

August 5, 2000
Mt. Morris, Michigan

A Backward Look

—— ﹏ 1 ﹋ ——

SURPRISE ELECTION

𝕴 was in Battle Creek, Michigan, when I got the phone call from Jim Bryan, executive director of the American Guild of Organists.

"Are you coming to the annual meeting in New York?"

"I'm not planning to."

"You'd better be here. I can't say any more right now."

"Oh, my God. I'll find a way to get there."

Earlier I'd had a phone call asking permission to put my name on the ballot as a candidate for national president of AGO. Nancy Phillips, who had recently moved from Washington, D.C. to a place in Connecticut near my hometown of New London, had become chair of the nominating committee for national officers. Nancy quoted various members around the country who were saying, "Those people in New York have been running things long enough—they don't know what it's like out here. Roberta does!" Furthermore, the top Guild officers had always been men. The committee itself was all male except for the chair, and so it was with "considerable trepidation," as she later said, that Nancy offered her proposal to nominate a woman for one of the top two slots. Nancy told them she had me in mind. To her amazement, the committee went for the idea. When she called to ask me, I told her to go ahead and put my name on the ballot—what could it hurt? But I didn't expect to get it.

I knew the mail-in ballots had already been counted when Jim Bryan called, and figured that the fifty or so ballots that would be cast at the annual meeting would probably not change the outcome.

3

My biggest problem was what to wear. It was mid-May, but fore-casts were for eighty-degree weather in New York. I had cool weath-er clothes suitable for New York but not hot weather clothes. I looked through my closet and pulled out the maroon outfit that had been designed and made for me especially for recital playing. It had a knee-length jacket that could be flipped behind the bench and slacks. I pulled out a white blouse instead of the heavier one that was made to go with the outfit. It turned out to be just right.

I arrived at St. Thomas Church a little early for the annual meet-ing and sauntered in casually. Some people were a little surprised to see me in New York—"all the way from Michigan"—but I sat there with my innocent face hanging out. It was fun being there when the vote counters came back into the room, and hearing the audible reactions of various people. Next day I learned that there were some in New York who had concerns about how I could possibly "run the Guild from the Midwest," but I had answers for all of them.

"You have one more minute." President Bitgood presides at a National Council meeting with gavel and finger-cymbals, ca. 1980. At left is AGO executive director Daniel N. Colburn II.

During the next six years, I traveled over 150,000 miles, 70,000 of them by car, visiting at least 125 AGO chapters, including one in Panama. If I had a date in a certain place, I would write to deans of nearby chapters to see if they also wanted me to come. I usually stayed with members in their homes rather than in hotels as my predecessors had done. Many Guild problems were thrashed out at kitchen tables after midnight.

On one trip to Evanston, Illinois, I had quite a surprise. The night before the chapter meeting I was there to attend, I went to a recital at a Baptist theological seminary. There on the beautiful four-manual organ was a bronze plate with the inscription "Given in memory of my father, Dr. William Howard Doane." This man, composer of the hymn "More Love to Thee, O Christ," was actually a relative of my father, and my uncle Doane Bitgood had been named for him. The Bitgood family had considered William Doane "a sissy" because he had gone away to college instead of staying back on the farm.

While I was Guild president, I took up needlepoint because I could do that on trains and planes. Over the years, I finished chair seats for four Victorian chairs that had belonged to my family, and also a piano bench cover.

During my first year as AGO president, I still worked at First Congregational Church in Battle Creek, but I managed to get back and forth to New York. On one trip I realized after I got to the airport in Detroit that I had forgotten to take the canoe off the top of my car. When I returned I discovered that it certainly did make the car easier to find in that mass of cars at Detroit Metro!

On another trip to AGO national headquarters, I could not avoid taking Stella, our beloved Weimaraner. We had inherited her from our daughter, Grace, in 1973. (The phone conversation went something like this: "Hello, Mother, you do love Stella, don't you?" "Yes, of course, why?" "Can you meet her at the airport on Saturday at 3:30?" Grace was leaving for a stint in Hong Kong and couldn't bear to give Stella to strangers.) By now, Stella had become part of the family. We were driving from Michigan via New Jersey to Connecticut, with a stop midway in New York for an executive meeting at

"On the road" with Stella, ca. 1977.

headquarters. Of course, I couldn't leave Stella locked in a hot car in the parking garage, so I asked if I could bring her to the meeting. The answer was, "Sure." She was a very well-behaved dog and so I knew I could do that. They sent me to the freight elevator with the dog. When we got to the twentieth floor, my hands were full and I had to let go of the leash. Stella entered headquarters first, with a loud bark, and checked out every room, barking as she went. Then from somewhere inside, a voice was heard to say, "Ah, the president has arrived!"

During those years, I closed every one of my speeches to local chapters with these words of Albert Schweitzer:

> *I am but one, but I am one.*
> *I cannot do everything, but I can do something.*
> *What I can do, I ought to do.*
> *And, what I ought to do,*
> *By the grace of God, I will do.*

෬

$\backsim 2 \backsim$

MUSIC LESSONS

Many years earlier, I'd had my first organ lessons at age fifteen from Mr. Howard Pierce. He was a volunteer orchestra director for the separate girls' and boys' high schools in New London, Connecticut. It was a big deal getting to do something with the boys two afternoons a week after school. So, on those afternoons, I trudged up the hill to Bulkeley, the boys' school, with my violin on my hip. Mr. Pierce was really a math teacher and didn't get paid for this extracurricular effort. I attended the girls' "college prep" school, Williams Memorial Institute, which in recent years moved its premises from the original building in downtown New London to a facility adjoining the Connecticut College campus.

One day, while I was at the Groton Congregational Church to rehearse a violin piece for a service the following Sunday, Mr. Pierce motioned me to the organ.

"Sit down and try it. It's fun."

"I don't know how," I said.

"Just try it—it's easy."

I sat down and poked around and found I could hit a pedal note once in a while. It was a broken-down tracker organ. Mr. Pierce had had polio as a child but was inspired to learn the organ by hearing the large concert organ in his hometown of Portland, Maine. He loved young people and did what he could to encourage them. He gave me two lessons and then asked me to substitute for him on the Sunday after Christmas so that he could go up to Portland for a visit. My family came across the Thames River on the ferry to hear me

PROGRAM

MUSIC, ... *School Orchestra*

MUSIC -- Speed Our Republic, . . . *Keller*
  SCHOOL CHORUS

CONCERT RECITATION -- The Creed of the Real
  American, ... *Crane*
  SCHOOL

MUSIC -- Invocation, ... *Hatton*
  SCHOOL CHORUS

COMPOSITION -- Oliver-Ellsworth, the Trusted
  Friend of Washington,
  VIRGINIA WEMPLE

MUSIC (a) Sing Again, Nightingale, . . *Zeller*
  (b) Fleecy Clouds, ... *Beethoven*
  GIRLS CHORUS, *violin obligato*, ROBERTA BITGOOD

FOUR MINUTE SPEECHES --
  Our Debt to the Immigrant,
  MILDRED BEEBE

  From Zahleh to New London,
  JAMES GORRA

MUSIC -- The Brotherhood of Man, . . . *Auber*
  SCHOOL CHORUS

ORAL COMPOSITION -- British East Africa,
  ALTA KNAPP

MUSIC (a) Summer will Come, . . . *Denza*
  (b) Shepherd Song, . . *Old French Melody*
  GIRLS CHORUS

RECITATION -- What Our Flag Means, . . *Lodge*
  GERARD MARIANO

MUSIC -- The Bells of Aberdovey, . *Welsh Melody*
  SCHOOL CHORUS

PRESENTATION OF DIPLOMAS,
  P. LE ROY HARWOOD
  President Board of Education

AWARDING OF PRIZES.

MUSIC, ... SCHOOL ORCHESTRA

MUSIC -- Star Spangled Banner, . . . *Key*

SALUTE TO THE FLAG.

MUSIC, ... SCHOOL ORCHESTRA

HONOR PUPILS

Abramson, Gertrude	Morrison, Felicite	Bauer, John
Beebe, Mildred	Mugovero, Alice	Beckwith, Raymond
Bitgood, Roberta	Paton, Elizabeth	Crawley, Willard
Cooper, Roberta	Sellew, Ruth	Cruise, Edward
DeLong, Ida	Smith, Beulah	DeGange, John
Hankey, Phyllis	Swanson, Bernhardina	Donovan, Kenneth
Kellogg, Ewart	Tanenbaum, Florence	Elder, Freeman
Kuriansik, Sarah	Wemple, Virginia	Eshenfelder, Henry
Lyons, Alice		Hoare, Leo
Meyers, Bessie	Ames, Franklin	Mariano, Gerard

Graduation exercises, Nathan Hale Grammar School, New London, Connecticut, June 30, 1920.

play, and one of them remarked with surprise that I sounded like "a regular organist." With this encouragement, and the offer of the church to give me a key so that I could come over on Saturday and Sunday afternoons to practice, I continued studying. The Methodist church in New London, where my family members were "pillars," had a fairly new Moller organ but church officials did not want "young girls" playing on "our beautiful new organ." So, thanks to Groton Congregational, I got started.

I did not have a strong piano background, and so I had to learn bass clef among other things. The violin had been my first instrument, at age five. I had seen a toy violin in a store. My mother believed the psychology book that said, "If you think your child is musical, expose her to music," and so she thought it better to buy me a real half-size violin.

An older man gave me my first violin lessons at his home in Norwich. While I played, he would go downstairs and saw wood. When my mother found out about it, that was the end of that. Mother then found a telephone operator in New London who also taught violin, named Margaret Coyle. Miss Coyle would come to our house to give me lessons. This woman knew how to teach.

I used to play my violin for various events and programs. I remember one occasion when I was playing for a group of people and my mother hadn't tuned my violin properly. I was incensed—"Put that violin away, I'm not playing it!"

We lived in downtown New London on Masonic Street, with my maternal grandparents. From there we could walk to most every place. Mother made sure she walked me to concerts and saw to it that I attended the vespers around the corner at St. James Episcopal Church, where I was always very impressed to hear the boys' choir perform. The little boys I knew as ruffians looked like little angels singing up there. Thanks to a wealthy member in the church, St. James had a wonderful four-manual Skinner organ. We attended the Methodist church on Sunday mornings, but the choir wasn't so good there. They had a soprano who sounded like a trumpet and a bass who sounded like a trombone. That was of course in the days of the

Fifty-Fifth Annual Meeting

NEW ENGLAND BRANCH
WOMAN'S FOREIGN MISSIONARY SOCIETY
METHODIST EPISCOPAL CHURCH

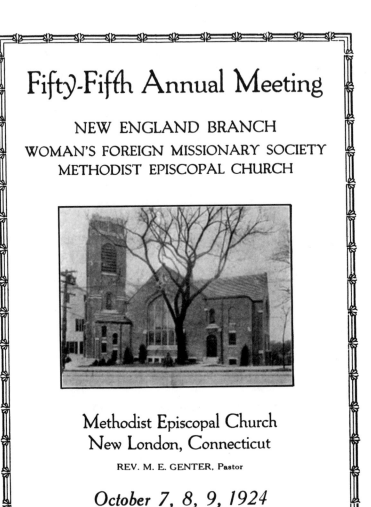

Methodist Episcopal Church
New London, Connecticut

REV. M. E. GENTER, Pastor

October 7, 8, 9, 1924

PROGRAM

MRS. F. H. MORGAN, Presiding

❦

TUESDAY, OCTOBER 7

Morning

10.00. Devotions. Mrs. A. E. Barber.
Home Base Conferences with Secretaries and Treasurers.

Afternoon

2.00. Departmental Conferences of Delegates and Secretaries.

Evening

YOUNG PEOPLE'S RALLY

Mrs. A. L. Lamont, Presiding

7.00. Devotions. Mrs. Harry I. Stoddard.

7.15. Address. Miss Bertha Starkey of Japan.

7.35. Greetings from our Standard Bearer Missionary. Miss Menia Wanzer of China.

7.45. Violin Solo. Miss Roberta Bitgood.

7.50. Foreign Students' Hour.

> Kitajima San . . . . Japan
> Ruth Ho . . . . China
> Mary Tang . . . . China
> Helen Kim . . . . Korea

8.25. Music.
Offering.

8.30. Musical Pageant.
Presented under the direction of Mrs. Robert A. T. Bitgood.
Benediction.

MUSIC

PIANO   .   .   .   .   Mrs. R. R. Abell

ORGAN .   .   .   .   Miss Roberta Bitgood
Mr. Howard T. Pierce

VIOLIN .   .   .   .   Miss Roberta Bitgood

SOLOS   .   .   .   .   Miss Leno e Elwood
Mrs. E. W. Jones

DUET .   .   .   .   Mrs. Marvin E. Smith
Mrs. Albert J. Hewitt

ORCHESTRA   .   .   .   .   .   .   W. M. I. and Bulkeley

Do not fail to visit the literature table. You will find helps for all kinds of missionary work, leaflets, demonstrations, pageants, songs, program suggestions and mite boxes.

11

Lorenz choir quarterlies. Later, when I became the assistant organist of our church, I took over the junior choir, whose members were not much younger than myself!

My grandparents always had an old upright piano. My mother had read about a method of teaching music that involved calling the notes by the names of animals: "Here is the pig, here is the monkey, here is the cow…" She soon realized that I could identify "the animals" without looking at the keyboard. This was long before anyone had heard of the Suzuki Method. It was my mother and my aunt, Marenda Prentis, who gave me my first piano lessons.

3

FAMILY PORTRAIT

My grandparents' home, where I was born, was a big, twelve-room, four-story, brick row house, and so there was room for my parents and me, and they always rented out rooms as well. The story goes that my father was originally living in a rooming house next door. One day, seeing my mother walk down the street, he remarked, "I'm going to marry that girl." He apparently took a room at my grandparents' in order to meet her. And so Robert Treat Bitgood, named after Connecticut's Governor Treat, did marry Grace Robinson Prentis, whose middle name was that of the Methodist minister who had married her parents.

My parents had a home wedding. A friend of the family played the piano, and Herbert Root, the Methodist minister who had originally been interested in my mother, officiated. Because her best friend, Winifred, had a crush on him, Mother had steered him in her direction.

My mother, Grace, was young when she married. If it hadn't been for that, she probably would have gone to college as her younger sister, my aunt Marenda, did. In those days, it wasn't the thing for housewives to do anything but keep house.

I arrived on the scene on January 15, 1908. The midwife was called to 19 Masonic Street. Another mother-to-be needed the midwife's services on the same day. So Huntington Byles and I shared the same birthday, and as it turned out, the same profession.

In my kindergarten year I attended public school. Because there were no crossing guards in those days, my mother walked me to and from school. When I moved up to the first grade, with school in session both mornings and afternoons, she would have had to walk me four times a day, so it was decided that I would go to a private school which met in the teacher's home. Some sort of health problem kept Miss Allen from going out, so that is why she had a "home school." The other students were from families who were fairly well-to-do, but the tuition at Miss Allen's school must not have been prohibitive. As a teacher, Miss Allen was inclined to push students if possible, so that is how I got ahead academically.

I have to say that my mother had a hard time letting me grow up. I had skipped two grades but she wanted me to look like girls my own age. So when I was in the fifth grade, she still wanted me to wear a big bow on the top of my head. I took it off on the way to school, and put it back on before I went home. I didn't want to be made fun of by the others in my class. Nor did I want to hurt my mother's feelings. By the time I hit high school, I finally went on strike about the hair ribbons.

"Young scholar," June 30, 1920.

My mother valued education and loved books. She was a fast reader—she could read half a page at a glance. My father wouldn't believe she was reading, but she really knew what she read. She liked mysteries. The librarian in New London used to give her new books to review before he shelved them, since he didn't have time to do it. My mother did have elocution lessons after her marriage, and she became a very good public speaker. She was much in demand as a speaker for the Home Missionary Society of the Methodist Church, and it was said that she could "draw money from a stone." She was a real bargain as a speaker because she had a railroad pass (thanks to my father's employment as a locomotive engineer) and therefore didn't need reimbursement for travel. My grandmother always took care of me while my mother went on those speaking engagements.

There was one occasion when my mother dressed up as a school-girl, in a pink gingham dress with a big hair-ribbon, and spoke in the first person to raise money for a certain orphanage in Kentucky. Prentis Hall was a dormitory at the Ritter Institution, so named in honor of my grandmother. I think she had been very active as a fundraiser before my mother. One of my mother's "lines" in this dramatic monologue was: "That name 'Prentis' sounds pretty good to me!" Everyone laughed at this reference to my mother's real identity.

One day, Mother came home from a church meeting and asked her parents what they thought was the greatest thing that could happen to her. They said, "To be elected as a delegate to the Methodist

Prentis family portrait. From left: Carrie Mason Prentis, Grace Robinson Prentis, Marenda Elliott Prentis, Stephen Avery Prentis, ca. 1905.

Engine 1409, Merchants Limited, Engineer Robert A.T. Bitgood, July 8, 1940. Bottom right: Robert Bitgood with Patrick McGinnis, president of New York, New Haven & Hartford Railroad, at a banquet held in honor of Bitgood's "fifty year run," 1951.

General Conference." They had guessed her surprise. She was the first woman ever elected to that position. She took it very seriously, attended every session, and came back and gave talks about it. Again, she was able to use her railroad pass to get to the meeting and back. Some of those trips were to quite distant places. I remember one meeting was held in New Mexico, and my mother brought back quite a few Navajo rugs.

My father worked on the New York, New Haven & Hartford Railroad, driving locomotive engines. Even though he had only a grade school education, he had a knack for memorizing the thick book of rules for railroad work. He had started out as a fireman but had advanced to the post of engineer faster than most men. When the company bigwigs needed an authority on rules, they often asked for my father. He would race home and put on a business suit before meeting with his bosses down in New Haven.

My father, Robert, had a certain amount of intuit.
engineer. At the time of the 1938 hurricane, he surprised
on his train by stopping suddenly. "Bob, you have a clear sig
are you stopping?" My father answered, "There's something w
ahead. I'm not moving." As they learned later, there was a brid,   at
up ahead, because of the hurricane, and the signals were out of order.
A train coming in the other direction had already gone into the
drink. There were people swimming around there, trying to recover
their suitcases.

Robert's people had been farmers in the Voluntown area of
Connecticut. The stepmother who brought my father up was a fairly
well-educated woman who was not thought of too highly by the family because she "always had her nose in a book." (That was probably

---

THE NEW LONDON, CONN., EVENING DAY, WEDNESDAY, MAY 9, 1951

Robert Bitgood, Veteran R. R. Engineer, Is Honored

Robert A. T. Bitgood of Best View, Waterford, who cherishes the memories of the days when he was at the throttle of steam engines when they pulled into Grand Central station, New York, has completed more than a half century of service with the New Haven railroad and this morning was presented a 50-year diamond studded pin in recognition of his long tour of duty.

"There aren't many who can still claim the distinction of taking a passenger train drawn by steam into Grand Central," he said in recalling his work in the early 1900's before the section of the road between New Haven and New York was electrified.

H. F. Donnelly, superintendent of the Providence division, presented the pin in a ceremony at Union station. Among those present was William J. Duggan, assistant superintendent of the Providence division, in whose office the presentation took place.

Fellow Employes Attend

Also among the 30 persons attending were fellow employes, Union station supervisors, representatives of railroad labor organizations, Bitgood's brother, J. P. Bitgood, of Waterford; his nephew, Royal E. Bitgood, of this city, and a close friend, Ernest Hester, Waterford.

Donnelly referred to Bitgood as a good engineer, "probably one of the best," and said his record is absolutely clear. He told Bitgood he will receive within a week a gold pass which will be good on all trains.

Duggan, recalling that he has known Bitgood since 1915, "when I hadn't even learned all the signals," said he could say nothing but the best of him and that he always has been very cooperative.

Prophecy Came True

Several others spoke, including Bitgood's brother, who told of an incident which occurred "many years ago when we were just youngsters." As they were working in the yard with their father the sound of a locomotive whistle was heard, he said, and his brother declared that some day he would be blowing that whistle.

Bitgood, a native of Voluntown, first took employment with the railroad Sept. 1, 1900 as a fireman. He was promoted to an engineer March 10, 1904, and operated passenger trains until Jan. 14, 1946, when he assumed the position of engineer on the local yard switcher.

Hesitant to discuss his long railroad career, Bitgood said he has operated some of the best trains on the road, including the Merchants Limited, which he was aboard about nine years.

Pin Presentation Ceremony

H. F. Donnelly, superintendent of the Providence division of the New Haven railroad, presents a 50 year diamond studded pin to Robert A. T. Bitgood of Best View, Waterford, during a ceremony this morning at Union station. Looking on is William J. Duggan, assistant superintendent of the Providence division, in whose office the ceremony took place.

© *The Day Publishing Co.*
Used with permission.

her escape!) Much later, I was often told (by Aunt Marenda, who sometimes had a caustic wit) to remember that I came from "a long line of circus material." On my father's side, everyone was stout and hefty. Robert's brother, my uncle Elmer, was even something of a legend in Connecticut. He had always competed in the county fair at lifting barbells and generally wanted to save his energy for that activity instead of farming. On one occasion, he was reported to have lifted a railroad car off its tracks by himself, and then wanted a hundred dollars to put it back.

Robert farmed until he was twenty-one and absorbed from the Bitgoods certain ideas about what women should and should not do. He probably never appreciated my mother's abilities as a public speaker, thinking that women should just stay at home and bake. He was not a churchgoer, and he once reacted bitterly when I asked if he would attend a neighbor lady's wedding. This incident gave me quite a shock. I should say that my father was not big on tenderness. Years later, my grandmother said to me, "I taught your mother to be long-suffering, but I should have taught her how to use a rolling pin!"

My mother's family were staunch Methodists. Grandfather Prentis had studied history and knew the story of John Wesley's heart being "strangely warmed" while embarked on an ocean-going vessel with a group of Moravians. He had heard them singing their beautiful chorales during a storm at sea. My grandmother, Carrie Mason Prentis, was very much against gambling and would not even buy "chances" from a boy who came to our door to raise money for his church. I thought at the time that she could have been a little less forceful about it. "Mater," as she was called, was also a rigorous supporter of prohibition.

I saw a picture once of Mater carrying a white flag and leading a group of people down State Street in New London. It was explained to me that she was leading a women's suffrage parade. So, besides coming from a line of "circus material," I am also descended from a line of strong-willed women.

The only pet I was allowed to have as a child was a turtle. A hole was drilled in the shell so that I could walk it around with a string for

*"Camp meeting
Sunday."
Methodist camp-
ground at
Willimantic,
Connecticut,
August 1931.
From left:
Stephen Avery
Prentis, Marenda
Elliott Prentis,
Grace Prentis
Bitgood, Carrie
Mason Prentis,
Roberta Bitgood.*

a leash. Mater was a very large woman and seemed to be terrified at
the notion of having an animal cause her to fall by getting underfoot.
One day, my grandfather brought home a puppy and she announced
in her stentorian tones, "Steve, either this puppy leaves or I leave!"
In my own adulthood, I have enjoyed my various pets.

One job I was given as a child was to take the weekly church bulletin over to a shut-in, Mrs. Baker, who lived at the Smith Memorial
Home. My folks had the idea that this older lady would enjoy having
a kid around sometimes, and indeed she did. I also walked along with
my grandfather out Broad Street to pay visits to his sisters, who were
always referred to as "the girls."

My grandfather Stephen Avery Prentis was a professional stonecutter. I remember him taking me out to the cemetery at times to see
certain stones that he had cut. In a town where there wasn't a lot to
do, I used to enjoy riding my bike out to the cemetery to feed the
ducks on the pond. I suppose some people played cards for amusement,
but to my Methodist family cards were the instrument of the devil.

Unions came in at a certain point and my grandfather (who was
himself a political independent) didn't believe in unions, so at last he
couldn't work as a stonecutter anymore. He then became the favorite
day watchman at the Brainard and Armstrong Silk Mill in New
London. He was reliable, and I believe they rather took advantage of

him. He wouldn't work on Sundays, but he worked on all the holidays—twelve-hour shifts, from six in the morning to six in the evening. I used to take over a big flat basket filled with a turkey dinner at twelve noon sharp on holidays, and he would come to the door to get it. I'd stay a while to sit with him while he ate. Otherwise, he spent the day making his rounds, checking every lock.

My grandparents were known to us as a devoted couple. I remember sometime in the late thirties walking to Grand Central Station and catching a 12:15 p.m. train out of New York after church to attend their 60th anniversary celebration. They had just moved into their new house at 240 Hempstead Street. Mater had always said, "Only the U.S. government will get me out of this house (the house on Masonic Street, which we had rented from the Smith Memorial Home)." And sure enough, the U.S. government did move my grandmother—they bought our place from Smith Memorial in order to build the New London Post Office, which stands there today as a special landmark for me. If not for that post office, my grandparents could never have bought their own home.

——— 4 ———

BEST VIEW

On a particular day early in their marriage, my parents took a trolley out to the edge of town and walked down a dirt road, past an empty cottage with the name "Best View" on it. The cottage overlooked the Thames River, and so they thought it really did have the best view anywhere around. They asked a farmer they saw working nearby if he knew who owned it.

"I do," was the reply.

"Can we buy it?" they asked.

"No, but you can lease it."

And so they did lease the cottage—for five years, after which the owner finally agreed to sell it to my parents.

Best View became my mother's salvation since in the winter they always lived with my grandparents. My father Robert built a sizeable swimming raft and a dock on the beach—partly because at low tide there was soft mud everywhere—and eventually he also built a small cabin down the bank by the water. In later years, this cabin became his home. I swam here from an early age. I have memories of

Roberta at play, Best View, ca. 1913.

Trolley stop at Best View, Quaker Hill, ca. 1910.

my mother entertaining many church groups at Best View too. The original cottage was an old-fashioned little house with no indoor plumbing.

We did not own a car then, and therefore depended on the trolley to get us back and forth between Best View and the family house in town. My mother didn't believe in taking the trolley on Sunday, and so in the summer we would walk the mile or so to the Quaker Hill Baptist Church, up the road from the cottage. One very hot Sunday morning when I was quite young, we had walked there to church and I fainted during the sermon. I was then carried out onto the lawn and someone volunteered a horse and buggy to take me home. After that incident, the rules were relaxed somewhat and we rode the trolley on Sunday, back to the Methodist church in town.

In 1916, my parents built a more elaborate house on the same site. The new house was a two-story brownshingle home with a veranda opening on three sides and a screened-in sleeping porch on the second floor. The "front" of the house, with the veranda and upstairs porch, faced onto the water instead of the street. This house continued to be a favorite spot for Sunday School picnics and a meeting place for the Home Missionary Society.

Although Best View was really a summer home, we also managed to live here in September and May with no heat. With my father at work on the railroad, my mother and I were alone in the house a great deal of the time. After I went to New York, I would sometimes bring friends back to Best View to visit, and later I used to bring my choir kids from New Jersey to stay down at the little cabin. This was quite a lark for some of those city kids and more informal than an organized camp.

The 1938 hurricane blew the little cabin down by the water over on its side. Robert took the trolley out to clean up, but when he saw it he decided to leave it just as it was and come back the next day.

Robert Bitgood, Smith Cove, Best View, ca. 1915.

When he did come back, he found that his brother Jesse, who at that time worked as head engineer at the Connecticut College power plant, had already put the cabin upright using what they called a "block and tackle." Those Bitgoods were ingenious and they were also strong. I suppose that Robert, in his own way, was also a dynamic person: he is still remembered by some around the Best View area for the way he organized the neighborhood boys to clean up after that hurricane.

After my daughter Grace arrived on the scene, I used to like to come back to Best View with her in the summer. I could get away from Westminster Presbyterian in New Jersey for a good part of the summer because all the churches in that area would get together and hold "union services," with different organists taking turns. That being the case, I enjoyed play-

Roberta with Carrie and Steve Prentis, Best View, ca. 1915.

The new house at Best View, ca. 1931.

ing in New London at the charming Pequot Chapel for ten weeks. My husband Bert was in the service then and my father Robert would entertain Grace while I was playing.

The Yale-Harvard boat race the third week in June used to be a big deal around here. People came from absolutely all over for it. Train cars appeared on both sides of the river and the seats were turned sideways. In later years, it was possible to drive down to the water to watch. I remember one summer when I was studying in New York, I had the job at First Presbyterian while Dr. Carl was in Europe. I would come home during the week and go down to New York to play on the weekends. The day of the boat race, I went out in my canoe to watch. Suddenly I heard a voice from one of the big, fancy yachts that was parked out there for the race: "Why, Roberta! Is that you? What on earth are you doing here?" One of the wealthy parishioners of First Presbyterian had discovered me in my natural habitat.

Over the years, many friends have enjoyed visits with us at Best View, some of them staying down the bank in the cabin. One family, the Calder Gibsons, had two little boys, who, seeing that there was only one bed down there, wondered where they were going to sleep. Some "bunk beds" were improvised for them, using dresser drawers.

In 1976, while I was in New York for one of those many Guild meetings, Bert had to make the decision to have the Best View house razed, due to the fact that termites had actually taken over even the cement blocks of the foundation. He was standing alongside the road waiting for me when I arrived at Best View, where now there was just a big hole in the ground. Only the old garage was still standing. The ground then had to be fumigated, and there was nothing to do after that but start over. A new house plan was drawn up by Bert and his brother-in-law, John Armstrong. This new house—the third to stand on this site—would finally become our retirement home.

Just at this time, my aunt Marenda Prentis, who had retired from her career in social work in Boston ten years before, had fallen at Harkness Chapel while attending a Connecticut College reunion weekend and had broken her pelvis. She needed a place to recover and it was decided that she should share our home, still then under construction. Bert showed her the house plans. She asked why there

Third house under construction, Best View, 1976. Bert and Marenda supervise.

was an extra bathroom on one end. Bert asked her, "Wasn't it you who said that anyone over the age of eighty ought to have her own bathroom?" Marenda choked up when she realized this was actually an invitation.

Later on, Marenda announced to us after she had moved in: "I've been living alone in Boston for fifty years. Now I've moved into a home with two adults, two dogs, and a cat. So I have a big adjustment to make!" My sweet husband then said under his breath: "My house, my dogs, my cat." Despite what some people referred to as her "formidable personality," Marenda always got along well with Bert, and he was always very nice to her. Marenda stayed at Best View until another fall at home made it necessary for her to have nursing home care.

Bert spent his last months here, too, in 1984, enjoying what he always called "the million-dollar view." He was suffering from cancer of the pancreas, and we had concealed the diagnosis from Grace. This was the time of her Ph.D. exams at Berkeley, and when she phoned to tell us she had passed, we had this sad news for her. She came east then to care for him at home. During this time, Bert's sister Greta, too, spent many weeks at Best View, helping us to make him more comfortable. At last in June, it was felt he needed hospice care, and so he moved to Branford, where we visited him daily.

Best View is still home for me and in some ways it seems strange to be back right where I started. Some people would think I keep it too cluttered, but I like to have things out that are meaningful to me. There's no sense having them tucked away in drawers. I never tire of sitting on the porch looking at this "best view" of all. There used to be a couple of houses across the cove that aren't there anymore. At some point a clubhouse was built on the opposite shore. It seemed to be a hangout for firemen. They had a player piano and you could hear it clunking away on summer evenings. More recently, you can see the Gold Star bridge off in the distance. And of course, the "Navy yard" is still there across the river—only now it's called the Groton Submarine Base. During World War II, they had to be careful about keeping the lights turned off.

Mamacoke Island—just outside the cove—is still owned by Connecticut College and they have chosen to keep it wild. The Central Vermont Railroad bridge, which separates our cove from the Thames, is not used much anymore. Passenger service was discontinued long ago and now there is only the occasional freight train. My father Robert used to refer to the Central Vermont line as "two streaks of rust and a right of way."

The trees going down the bank now block our view in certain places—you have to go almost to the corner of the lot to get a clear view. I remember my mother, years ago, standing at the top of the hill, directing Robert about where to trim off the branches. "There! There! And now over there!" But despite the overgrowth, I feel lucky to still be in my own home.

⸎

5

CONNECTICUT COLLEGE

𝕴 started as a violin major at Marenda's alma mater, Connecticut College, but I wasn't the "Joe College" that she was. She had more school spirit in her little finger than I could muster altogether. She had had to "kill time" for three years until the college opened. Her mother had said, "There's going to be a college here and you are going to go to it." So she taught at East Greenwich Academy while she waited for the school to open.

Roberta on campus, ca. 1926.

I was a commuter and went dutifully to everything, but I didn't like to hang around the campus with those "silly girls." I was something of a misfit in college, being two years younger than the others. I hid my grades because I didn't want anyone to see my straight A's.

As a sophomore, I decided I wanted to be an organ major. By this

𝔐𝔢𝔱𝔥𝔬𝔡𝔦𝔰𝔱 𝔈𝔭𝔦𝔰𝔠𝔬𝔭𝔞𝔩 ℭ𝔥𝔲𝔯𝔠𝔥
NEW LONDON, CONN.

SECOND ORGAN RECITAL

BY

ROBERTA BITGOOD

ASSISTED BY THE

CONNECTICUT COLLEGE CHOIR

ON THURSDAY, NOVEMBER 17, 1927, AT 8.15 P. M.

PROGRAM

1. Third Sonata in C-minor (Op. 56) . . . . *Guilmant*

    Preludio

    Adagio

    Fuga

2. (a) Music When Soft Voices Die . . . . *Dickinson*

   (b) At Eventide It Shall Be Light (Holy City) *Gaul*
       CONNECTICUT COLLEGE CHOIR

3. (a) Procession du St. Sacrement in A . . . *Chauvet*

   (b) Larghetto in F ♯ minor . . . . *Wesley*

   (c) Prelude and Fugue in C . . . . *Bach*

4. Draw Us to Thee . . . . *Barnes*
       THE CHOIR

5. (a) Pastorale in E . . . . *Franck*

   (b) Meditation in A♭ . . . . *Klein*

   (c) Intermezzo in B♭ minor . . . . . . *Callaerts*

   (d) Anniversary March in F . . . . *Erb*

Organ recital, 1927.

The college graduate, 1928.

time I had taken several lessons from Mr. Pierce, who after all was a "one-footed organist," so of course I played with one foot too. It was funny. He'd had polio, but it was his bad leg that he was using to play the pedals. He did have a natural ability and was actually employed at both the Groton Congregational and New London Methodist churches. I eventually became his assistant, to handle the junior choir and Sunday morning services at the Methodist church.

I went to Dr. J. Lawrence Erb, head of the music department and the organ teacher at the college, and asked to switch my major from violin to organ. He made it conditional—I had to take piano lessons as well. I drove Mr. William Bauer, the piano teacher, almost crazy because I could sight-read almost anything, but with dreadful finger-ing. He could not get over my right thumb being double-jointed. Violin lessons may have helped my "ear and musicianship," but they did not help me learn the bass clef. Soon, however, Mr. Bauer did put me into a student recital, saying, "Look what I have done with this student—in only two months!" For me, it was fun to be a "freak." And when I took the Guild exams much later, I could deal with the "open score" much better than some who had been "proper piano students." But when I started studying the organ with Dr. Erb, I did have my moment of truth—I had to learn to play with two feet.

Dr. Erb was a native of Brooklyn. The job he'd had before com-ing to Connecticut College was at the music school in Urbana, Illinois. He had written a theory book that was only about a half-inch thick. I liked that. The ones that are three inches thick—you can't possibly digest all that detail. But with him, everything was very concise. In Theory I, we used Dr. Erb's book, and there wasn't so much material there that you couldn't sort out the important stuff from the less important. I had felt somewhat abused, having to go to Connecticut College, because I would have liked better to have gone away to school. I'd had Syracuse in mind. Attending "CC" turned out to be a blessing in disguise, however, because of my theory study with Dr. Erb.

_____ ꙅ **6** ꙅ _____

WHEELS

The trolley was the way we got around when I was young. Trolleys were in considerable use before buses came in. The fare was five cents, or we could get six tokens for a quarter. Around the time of World War I, the price went up to ten cents.

I took the trolley to Norwich for my first violin lessons, and later to Connecticut College during my first two years. They ran frequently so it was convenient. It wasn't unheard of then for girls to travel around alone, which it might have been a generation before me.

There were two stops at Connecticut College and the next one was Thames View. At that point, there were double tracks and the trolley driver would wait there for the trolley going the other way to pass. There was nothing quieter than sitting there waiting, but when the other trolley arrived, you would have to shout to be heard. If you lived between stops and were on good terms with the motorman, he would let you out by your door.

When we were at Best View in the summer, sometimes our groceries arrived by trolley, too. We could order them from Mr. Gager, who lived near us and owned a nice market downtown, at the corner of Main and State streets. If we phoned before lunch, he would bring the groceries with him on the trolley when he came home at noon. That was handy.

As a junior at Connecticut College, I bought my first car, with my Sunday earnings, and suddenly became very popular. The girls who lived on campus were not allowed to have cars. I was the first person in my family to drive and to own one, and it was gorgeous! It was a tan convertible with green wheels, one of the last Model T's. They were being sold off before the Model A's came out, and I think I paid two or three hundred dollars for my "roadster." When I graduated from college, I didn't take the car to New York immediately. By then, I had taught my mother to drive, and she needed the car to transport my grandmother around.

On weekends during the summer, however, when I went to New York to substitute for my teacher, I would take my car. One time when I had parked it on the street in front of my girlfriend's apartment on 12th Street, I found no top on the car next morning. Somebody who evidently had the same model car had thought this was a good chance to get a new top. So, for a while, I had everybody in New York amused, because if it was raining I would hold an umbrella over my head. I had to keep the rain off of my face or I couldn't see. People thought that was quite funny! It probably was quite a picture to see me driving up and down Fifth Avenue like that. I was advised to go to all the junkyards to look for a replacement top. I finally did find a respectable-looking one.

Many people thought it was crazy to have a car in New York, because it was expensive to pay for a garage, but at some point it

Roberta and her Model T, "Daisy."

33

seemed worth it to me. That way, I gained some of my independence back. I was like a different person with wheels. And it was certainly more pleasant to travel by car than on a crowded subway.

It was especially good when I took a job in Bloomfield, New Jersey. I commuted two or three days a week for choir rehearsals, as well as on Sunday, and continued to live with my girlfriend in the apartment on 12th Street. At that point I couldn't stand the idea of being watched every minute as a single person in a folksy community such as Bloomfield. I would usually take the car ferry because it was only fifty cents as opposed to a dollar for the tunnel, and also it was enjoyable. There were always a few sights to see on the Hudson River. I'd commute uptown to Columbia a couple of days a week also, and take the road along the river if it was a nice day. I liked driving through Central Park too.

During the war, when driving was restricted, I kept a church bulletin on the seat so that I could prove I was driving to my job. Bert and I took my car on our honeymoon, which didn't last long because of the inevitable Sunday morning—I didn't take Sundays off in those days. Later, when I got my first hardtop sedan, I felt I had given up my youth—a first step toward being old!

7

GRADUATE WORK

finished college in 1928—at age twenty—a child wonder, you understand. It was an outdoor graduation. I was sitting up front in the choir. My mother, having seen the printed program before I did, mouthed the word "Everything!" to me, indicating I'd won both general and departmental honors.

I was starry-eyed because my organ teacher had those magic letters "FAGO"—Fellow of the American Guild of Organists—after his name. He gave me some old AGO examination papers to study, and I can remember thumping away at them on our old piano here at Best View. It seemed that I could do some of it. Dr. Erb knew I was interested in taking the AGO exams. Studying these old exams at the cottage was something I'd do in the summertime when not much else was going on up here.

Dr. Erb suggested that I apply for a scholarship at the Guilmant Organ School, which was then located at First Presbyterian Church in New York City. My mother loved New York and had taken me there as a little kid. Though she hated to lose me, she encouraged me to apply, and I did get a scholarship from an endowment made by one of Dr. William C. Carl's earlier students.

Room and board were of course going to be a big expense. My aunt Marenda noticed an ad in one of her social work magazines: "Pianist needed for large settlement house in New York. Call such-and-such a number." Marenda said, "Why don't you follow up on this?" So I did. Come to find out, the head worker was then at a summer camp in Stepney, Connecticut, not too far from New Haven, so

Roberta demonstrates the violin for a kindergarten group at Horace Mann School, 1932.

I went over there to be interviewed. Everyone was gathering around, expecting her to ask me to play. When she saw what my credentials were, it was settled without an audition that I would come to New York and move into the settlement house, where I would play for singing games, club meetings, and folk dancing in exchange for my room and board.

I knew settlement houses through Marenda, who had worked at two of them in Boston, where I had visited her. Again, my mother encouraged me and even rode the train with me the first time I went down to the settlement house. She still had her railroad pass and would often come to visit—sometimes unexpectedly—during the years I was there. Even though she let me go willingly, I think it really broke her heart when I went to New York, because I was the one bright spot in her life. A few years later, sad to say, she was hospitalized for a mental breakdown, never to return home again.

It was a little bit hard at the settlement house. I was on duty five afternoons a week starting at about four o'clock, and on Saturday mornings. I had a roommate who wanted to go to bed at eight or nine, so I always worked on music theory at the kitchen table, where I would not bother anyone by having the light on. One night, I was walking back from the subway at about 11 p.m., and I ran into one of the settlement house kids. I asked why he was out at that hour, and he replied, "Oh, my mother is 'borning' again, and they kicked me out."

East Side Settlement House was on 76th Street and overlooked the East River—another million-dollar view—in a poor neighborhood, but the fancy apartment houses were coming closer. The East River Drive went right up past it. They had to sell out at the end of that year.

Dr. William C. Carl, my teacher at the Guilmant School, was big on "drop, lift"—the *portato* touch—which I'd never heard of before. He also encouraged students to go out and visit choir rehearsals. I did this for six months, from September to March. The place I most liked to visit was St. Bartholomew's. They had a paid choir of sixty voices. Visitors were welcome at the Wednesday night rehearsals, but not at the Friday rehearsals. I figured there must be something going on at

Dr. William C. Carl at the Roosevelt console, First Presbyterian Church, New York. Photo courtesy of Agnes Armstrong.

those Friday rehearsals that the director—David McK. Williams— didn't want anybody to hear, so I used to sneak into them and lie down in the third pew.

Other students did this too. One time, a Navy man who had been working on a 48-hour shift went to visit the Friday night rehearsal at St. Bartholomew's. He fell asleep in one of the pews and didn't wake up until the rehearsal was over and the church was locked. I guess he had quite a time crawling in the pitch dark to a choir door exit.

In March of that year, 1929, I landed my first church job in New York, at First Presbyterian, where Dr. Carl was the organist. The job was to direct a junior choir and a mixed glee club, and to play for the Sunday School and the weekday noon-hour worship services, which were mostly attended by businessmen. This freed up Dr. Carl so that he could go out for lunch during the week, and also allowed him to "sleep in" on Sunday with a clear conscience.

I also landed a job at the First Moravian Church quite by accident, after substituting for someone who was going away. They paid forty dollars a month and the Presbyterian Church paid twenty-five. Through this job, I was introduced to the Moravian hymnal with its

Roberta with the First Presbyterian junior choir and mixed glee club, ca. 1930. Photo courtesy of Florence and Harold Miller.

First Presbyterian Church, New York, 1931.

nine hundred and fifty beautiful hymns. I later wrote my thesis at Union Seminary on Moravian music.

I also practiced at the Moravian Church, where the temperature in the winter was often 50 degrees or less. I warmed my hands over a radiator. I grew fond of the Moravians even though the Erben tracker organ was falling apart. It was probably the worst organ in New York City. I had to avoid using the swell to great coupler. Some of the pipes didn't work, and when there was a cipher the pipe had to be pulled. The historic value of this organ was later discovered and it was restored twenty years after I left.

I had joined the Guild as soon as I got to New York, because I thought it was important. There had not been a chapter anywhere around New London. Dr. Carl was, of course, active in the Guild. AGO members were considered the "academic organists." There was also the NAO—National Association of Organists. Dr. Carl said that it was a good idea to belong to both. At that time, in the 1920s, the Guild didn't hold conventions as the NAO did. And the people who founded the NAO—like Reginald McCall, for instance—weren't

THE PIRATES OF PENZANCE

or, The Slave of Duty

By

W. S. GILBERT and ARTHUR SULLIVAN

AT FIRST PRESBYTERIAN CHURCH
Thursday, April 23, 1936

Staged by DOROTHY MacLAUGHLIN

Musical Direction by ROBERTA BITGOOD

THE CAST

MAJOR-GENERAL STANLEY	WARREN MacNERNEY
THE PIRATE KING	BEN SHERER
SAMUEL, *his lieutenant*	GEORGE MADISON
FREDERIC, *the pirate apprentice*	HAROLD E. MILLER
SERGEANT OF POLICE	WILLIAM G. COLE
MABEL	ROBERTA ROBERTS
EDITH *General Stanley's Daughters* . . .	GRACE BRADFIELD
KATE	AURELIA LENCZOWSKA
ISABEL	JANETTE A. PIERCE
RUTH, *pirate maid of all work*	MINNIE M. HAUPTMANN

Chorus of General Stanley's Daughters: Alice Shahboz, Joyce Swift, Eleanor Mare, Catherine Carstensen, Lillian Carstensen

Choruses of Pirates and Police: Kirk Cramer, John H. Fischbach, Robert Daly, Joseph Rowan, James Best, Bill Cole

ACT I. A rocky seashore on the coast of Cornwall.

ACT II. A ruined chapel by moonlight.

Accompanist	CLIFFORD E. BALSHAW
Stage Manager	HARRIET A. BRADFIELD
Properties	MARGARET BURR
Costumes	FLORENCE WEISS
Make-up	GLADYS SIPPOLA

Appreciation is due the Madison Square Boys' Club for cooperation.

COMING EVENTS

COLLEGE CLUB DANCE .... Thursday, April 30th

SPRING FEVER FROLIC .... Friday, May 8th interested in the Guild exams. They were interested in a more social kind of organization. Later on the AGO started having conventions too. But conventions didn't cost so much then, and you could go to two in one summer.

Dr. Carl believed in the AGO exams, and his "little routine" was to have Guilmant students take the Associateship exam after their second year of study. The thing that Dr. Carl did not understand was that I, being a college music major, had a lot more background than some of his kids who came to his school right out of high school. So I had to fight Dr. Carl and some of the others, because "it takes two years to get ready for that."

Warren Hedden—who was, shall we say, a slightly disgruntled church musician but a whiz at theory—was the official theory teacher at Guilmant. Well, the first thing Mr. Hedden did with me was to say, "You're not going to sit through this stuff with these kids. Here, you come at such-and-such a time." He pushed me right into stuff he couldn't push the others into as fast. So, over Dr. Carl's

First Moravian Church, Lexington Avenue and 30th Street, New York, 1932.

41

objections, I took that Associateship exam after my first year and passed with higher marks than any of his other students at that time.

The next year, I moved to University Settlement House down on the Lower East Side, doing much the same kind of thing I had done the year before. The head worker of that settlement house was some-one Marenda had known in Boston. I had a little room right next to his apartment, and he had a grand piano that I could use to work on my theory.

That year Mr. Hedden said, "Oh, you're ready to take the Fellow-ship examination."

"Oh, Dr. Carl doesn't want me to take that."

Dr. Carl had told me how many years this one and that one (whom I would just as soon not name) had taken to pass the Fellow-ship exam. But I just kept listening to my theory teacher and going ahead with all the exercises. He gave me what amounted to private lessons, because, as he said:

"You don't need to be bored with all this stuff I have to give these kids—you do so-and-so."

We used good old Ebenezer Prout as a theory text, which was three inches thick, with a great deal of detail. There were pages and pages about the first inversion. Well, I didn't need pages and pages of it to learn how to use it. I was glad I had had Dr. Erb's book first, because that made it easier for me to absorb it all. With Mr. Hedden egging me on, and Dr. Carl slightly disapproving of my doing it, I took the Fellowship exam in New York a year after I'd taken the Associateship exam. It was 1930.

The program at the settlement house had finished up by then, so I was staying in New London during the weeks that summer. I was hoping for a letter about the results of the exam and I called the set-tlement house from New London to ask, "Is there any mail for me from the American Guild of Organists?"

"Yes."

"Would you please open it and read it to me?"

"Well, there are two columns of figures here. One at the bottom says, 'Practical—congratulations—pass: 85.'"

Guilmant Gold Medal awarded to Roberta Bitgood, 1930. Photos courtesy of Agnes Armstrong.

"OK, is there another column there?"

"Yes, there's another column over there that says, 'Theory—congratulations—pass: 85.'"

"Are you sure it's 85 under both columns?"

"Yes."

"OK, thank you very much. I'll be along in a little while."

Then I called Dr. Carl.

"This is Roberta Bitgood."

"Oh, did you have a nice time in Connecticut?"

After he stopped talking, I said, "I passed the Fellowship exam with 85 on both sides."

Dead, dead silence.

Then, "What did you say?"

"I think you heard me—the Fellowship, on both sides—85."

He had told me about the grades of some of his former students who were a little on the famous side, you know. But the thing he did not understand was that a college graduate who'd had a good theory teacher was going to start off knowing something. And of course, he was probably starting everybody else from scratch.

By the time I reached my destination, he'd called everybody in New York City.

"My student did this and that . . ."

It was just very funny. He got very excited about it.

Later, as a student at the Union Theological Seminary School of Sacred Music, I studied with Clarence Dickinson. He put the soul back into my playing. Dr. Carl's specialty was technique and Dr. Dickinson's was repertoire. He was a pioneer in his time, greatly elevating the level of church music. He also emphasized oratorio accompaniments.

I finished my master's degree at Union in 1935 and wanted to study with David McK. Williams. I had heard that he didn't like "lady pupils." To my surprise, he overheard me saying this at some event or other and came over and put his hand over my mouth.

"Why do you want to study with me? Come in some afternoon and we'll talk about it."

Dr. Williams was considered "low church." I seldom missed his evening vespers, but I had to make an extra trip over to talk to him.

I told him, "I like what you do, and I'd like it if a little rubbed off on me."

℘

∽ 8 ∾

BLOOMFIELD

hurches were *always* looking for a man! I'll describe the big, 1,500-member Presbyterian church job that I landed in Bloomfield, New Jersey. I wrote a letter of application—I had my credentials. Charles Poling was the minister, a brother of *the* Daniel Poling—one of the free spirits of a well-known family of ministers and theologians. They auditioned a lot of applicants—I don't know whether it was 50 or 150—and Dr. Poling liked the sound of my letter because I mentioned my interest in children's choirs. I had a children's choir in New York at the First Presbyterian Church and I was interested in oratorio. I knew they always had a solo quartet at this church and I looked forward to the opportunity of working with some of these fine singers, without whom you couldn't do oratorio work.

Well, Dr. Carl made me go through the agency—that's how honest he was. One of his students who was older than I—she had studied with him

Roberta on the Westminster steps, May 1932.

Westminster Presbyterian Church, Bloomfield, New Jersey.

years before—knew that the job was vacant. She had gotten him to write a letter for her. He didn't think she'd get it, but he wasn't dishonest enough to just come out and tell me about the job. So he made me go to the agency, saying, "Don't you leave that office until you get the name of that church!"

Bloomfield was Dr. Carl's hometown. And this woman who had studied with him evidently was not his most brilliant student, but she knew about the vacancy.

He wrote as best he could about her. But then he thought that maybe this was the kind of thing I could get because I directed the junior choir at his church there. Dr. Carl subsequently must have written a pretty good letter for me, because I got a call from Dr. Poling.

"Can you come out this afternoon?"

"Well, I don't know."

"Well, I'll tell you. The committee has it down to six men."

I never figured it out. One of my classmates at Union Seminary later said, "How did you get that job?" He was one of the six and he was a good musician.

But anyway, I said, "Fine, I'll come out this afternoon."

When I mentioned this to Dr. Carl, he said, "Now wear that blue dress and keep your hat on. That'll make you look older."

When I was 22, people always said I looked 16. Well, that turned out to be the first and last time I ever played an audition with a hat on!

I had my little Ford and I drove over there. I had just finished memorizing the Bach D Major, so I was thundering away at top speed. Evidently the minister went down to the secretary and said, "Boy, that baby sure can play!"

He then asked me a million questions about my feelings about a junior choir. Well, the first job I had had in New London was with a relatively junior or grown-up junior choir, so I was quite accustomed to working with those ages.

Then there was a millionaire in the congregation who had made the four-manual Odell organ possible. It was said that he "wouldn't take a woman" for the music position.

Dr. Poling asked after my audition, "Can you come out Sunday night to play? Can you come Sunday morning?"

He gave me bus fare, not realizing that I would drive my own car, and I got a substitute at the Moravian Church for Sunday so that I could go back out there. The millionaire came and liked what he heard and I landed the job. I was given a contract with a three-month termination notice and stayed fifteen years, from 1932 to 1947.

Roberta Bitgood (center front) with solo quartet and adults, junior and youth choirs at rear. Christmas carol service, Westminster Presbyterian Church, 1932.

News of the American Guild of Organists

Beautiful Service at Bloomfield Led by Roberta Bitgood

Following is the program of a musical service of the Union-Essex Chapter held at the Westminster Presbyterian Church, Bloomfield, N. J., Jan. 13: Psalm-Prelude, No. 1 (Psalm 34:6), Bach; "Great and Glorious" (Psalm 93), Dickinson; "By Babylon's Wave" (Psalm 137), Gounod; "Hear Ye, Israel" (Isaiah 48, 53, 49, 41, 51), Mendelssohn; "I Will Lift Up Mine Eyes" (Psalm 121), Sowerby; "Like as the Hart" (Psalm 42), Novello; "Comfort Ye" and "Every Valley" (Isaiah 40), Handel; "Lift Up Your Heads" (Psalm 24), Handel; "Thus Saith the Lord" and "But Who May Abide" (Haggai 2, Malachi 3), Handel; "I Waited for the Lord" (Psalm 40), Mendelssohn; Offertory, Andante (Third Sonata), Mendelssohn; hymn, "Our God, Our Help in Ages Past" (Psalm 90); "Beneath the Shadow of the Great Protection," Dickinson; "The Greatest of These" (I Corinthians, 13), Bitgood; "Praise Thou the Lord" (Psalm 103), Mendelssohn; "Bless the Lord, O My Soul" (Psalm 103), Ippolitoff-Ivanoff; "Alleluia! O Praise Ye the Lord" (Psalm 150), Franck; Benediction and Response, Handel; postlude, Toccata, "Thou Art the Rock" (Psalm 31:3), Mulet.

The service, of unquestioned reverence and aspiration, was under the direction of the organist, Miss Roberta Bitgood, M. A., F. A. G. O., M. S. M. It was a carefully-planned musical program, beautifully sung and competently accompanied. The choir sang with a depth of feeling and with fine tone control, reflecting the hard work and musicianship of the director. The quartet of soloists not only rendered their solos beautifully, but had an equally good ensemble. A number that impressed many because of the lovely way in which it was presented was Miss Bitgood's own composition, "The Greatest of These."

Miss Bitgood presides at an organ of worshipful tonal qualities and has a responsive and well-balanced choir and a quartet of solo voices of impressive beauty.

After the service chapter members wended their way to the First Baptist Church, where a demonstration of the new Hammond electronic organ was given by Lester B. Major, organist of the church.

I. HAMILTON, Registrar.

ROBERTA BITGOOD

AGO *column from* The Diapason, *1936.*

WESTMINSTER ORGANIST GIVES NEW HAVEN RECITAL

Miss Roberta Bitgood, organist and director of music at Westminster Presbyterian Church of Bloomfield, was one of the guest organists chosen to play one of a series of Lenten recitals in Trinity Episcopal Church of New Haven, Conn. The organ is a large new Aeolian-Skinner, which was formally dedicated last November. This historic church is one of the three on the "green" in that city. Miss Bitgood's recital there was on March 5th.

New Haven recital, ca. 1935.

There were probably some other people who had auditioned for the Westminster job who were as competent as I was, but then they hadn't done quite as many things. Of course, when I told them that it was unusual to have passed the Fellowship exam at the age of twenty-two, that kind of impressed them.

I still lived in the New York apartment with my girlfriend Lillian Mecherle, not too far west of Fifth Avenue, and made the trip out to New Jersey several times a week. Even when I didn't have my car in New York, I could walk to the Bowery late in the evening and be safe. I walked from 12th Street to 23rd Street and paid twenty-five cents to take the ferry over to New Jersey. When I did have my wheels, some of those biddies at Westminster Church would see me after choir rehearsal getting into my car at 9:30 and starting for New York.

"Oh, my husband wouldn't allow me to drive in New York, even in the daytime!"—and so on.

It didn't occur to me that this was strange, because once I had started driving, I drove everywhere around New London at night, and I think that New York wasn't quite the dangerous place it is today.

I was also attending Columbia Teachers' College at this time—I was nuts for going to school—and once I'd finished at the Guilmant School, my wise mother had said, "You'd better see if you can get a teaching degree. You'll always play the organ, but you might need to get a teaching job."

By this time, I was finishing my second year at Teachers' College and I didn't understand why people were jumping out of 27-story windows at the time the Depression hit. Having come from a humble family that was never rich, I couldn't understand how people could be so alarmed that they'd want to end it all in such a way. I could get along on my little shoestring. I had started at Teachers' College when I was still living at University Settlement House.

I also had the fun of playing violin in the Columbia University Orchestra with Douglas Moore conducting. This was a better orchestra than I'd ever played in before. The night I graduated from Columbia, I had to scurry to pick up my diploma in the office and then dash down to catch the ferry in order to get to a prayer meeting

Mikado accompanist and music director,
Mary Elizabeth Compton and Roberta
Bitgood.

at Westminster. I commuted like this for two years.

I think the first apartment I got in Bloomfield—once I finally broke down and moved over there—was something like thirty-five dollars a month. It was here that I had my first pet. I inherited a black cat named Satan. I started out with a borrowed upright piano. Then, when somebody needed to go to Florida, I acquired a baby grand for fifty dollars. The apartment was about a block from the church, and I used to warm up the choir there because a Sunday School class met in the only room with a piano at the church.

Charles Poling was enthusiastic about everything I did. But then he left. The new minister, whom they brought in from Steubenville, Ohio, was named Raymond Smiley. He didn't like anything I was doing, but he thought I could play. He liked the soloists, but he didn't like the choir. The chairman of the music committee came in on a rehearsal night in January of that particular year, because the minister wanted to get rid of the choir. He came in three months before they were supposed to quit—the first of May, you see—to tell them that their services weren't going to be needed any longer. In the meantime I had built up some personal loyalties—we'd worked on some oratorios. So after this, I said, "Well, whatever happens, if you'll stick by, I'm going to keep this choir going and if they don't want us to sing here, we can go out and sing other places." I had some pretty good singers there. One of the earlier ministers had started a chorus, which is what I had inherited along with the paid soloists.

By this time I was at Union Seminary, studying oratorio accompaniments. Finally, they let me do something with the choir once every two months on a Sunday night, when they thought nobody would come. But here I had all these top-notch soloists—because I would audition. I'd get "spies" working for me, to send me some of the best new students who had just come to Juilliard from the Midwest. I had some dandies. I lost two of them to the Met auditions. They were thrilled to death to have a chance to do oratorio work. They had just an hour's bus trip to get out there. I think they had to make two trips a week. So, with those fine singers around, other choirs liked to sing with us—works like the *St. Matthew Passion*. I had the soloists and so I'd say, "Well, you learn the first chorus parts and we'll learn the second chorus parts and then we'll put it all together." We had a ball! We put it on in three places, I think. Whether anyone ever liked it, I don't have any idea!

But people came from distances to hear these things, because I was the only one around there who had this caliber of soloists all the time. One of them, a tenor, was a schoolteacher in the area who had studied quite a bit. The ones who lived in New York had to sing for me Sunday nights, too, so they'd hang around my house in the after-

Mikado production, Bloomfield College and Seminary, May 1939. Photo above: Dorothea Wiersma and Roberta Bitgood (center left and right).

51

— PATRONS —

Dr. and Mrs. Joseph Hunter

Dr. and Mrs. John Dikovics

Professor and Mrs. Frank Kovach

Professor and Mrs. John Slater

Professor and Mrs. Franz Zeller

Professor Harry T. Taylor

Mrs. Elsa M. Andrew

Mrs. Emilie C. Berger

Rev. and Mrs. B. Pascale

Rev. and Mrs. Remi Buttinghausen

Mr. Daniel Mancini

Mr. and Mrs. Albert Bosshard

•

The Choir and Glee Club extend their thanks to the following Committees and to all others who contributed to the Production of this Operetta.

Properties and Stage .... Richard Kolozsar, Victor Turdo

Stage Director .... Lewis N. Raymond

Costumes .... Roberta Kovach, Mary Pipezio

Make-up .... Donald Scott (Courtesy of Elm Players, Montclair),
Kenneth Howat

Business Manager .... Robert B. Ackerman

Ushers .... Edith Dezso, Carole Politi

The Choir and Glee Club

of

Bloomfield College and Seminary

present

The

Mikado

or

THE TOWN OF TITIPU

by

GILBERT AND SULLIVAN

Friday, May 5th, 1939

•

FIRST PRESBYTERIAN CHURCH AUDITORIUM

Bloomfield, New Jersey

THE MIKADO OR THE TOWN OF TITIPU

CAST OF CHARACTERS

❦

The Mikado of Japan .... Emil Todaro
Nanki-Poo (his son, disguised as a Wandering Minstrel and in love
with Yum-Yum) .... Peter Boreyko
Ko-Ko, Lord High Executioner .... Ralph Keppel
Poob-Bah, Lord High Everything Else .... Ansley G. Van Dyke
Pish-Tush, a Noble Lord .... Donald Wilson
Yum-Yum ⎫ .... Alba Pascale
Pitti-Sing ⎬ Wards of Ko-Ko .... Dorothea Wiersma
Peep-Bo ⎭ .... Mary E. Morgan
Katisha (an Elderly Lady, in love with Nanki-Poo) ... Mary Piperio

Chorus of School Girls:

Edith De Rogatis, Rose Capua, Roberta Kovach, Patricia Kopf, Betty Hoelzer, Adele Liebig, Doris Fern, Charlotte Zeller, Clelia Moncada.

●

Director

Roberta Bitgood

Chorus of Notables:

Robert B. Ackerman, Frank Kish, Eugene Rose, Robert Murphy, David De Rogatis, Richard Koleszar, Benjamin Ashton, Stephen Feke, Winfield Ramish, Joseph Curto.

●

Accompanist

Mary Elizabeth Compton

Scene

●

THE GARDEN OF KO-KO'S OFFICIAL RESIDENCE

ACT 1

Musical Numbers

1. If You Want to Know Who We Are .... Chorus of Men
2. A Wandering Minstrel I .... Nanki-Poo and Chorus
3. Our Great Mikado .... Pish-Tush and Chorus
4. Young Man, Despair .... Pooh-Bah, with Nanki-Poo and Pish-Tush
5. And Have I Journeyed for a Month .... Nanki-Poo and Poo-Bah
6. Behold the Lord High Executioner .... Ko-Ko and Chorus
7. I've Got a Little List .... Ko-Ko and Chorus
8. Comes a Train of Little Ladies .... Chorus of Girls
9. Three Little Maids from School .... Yum-Yum, Pitti-Sing, Peep-Bo and chorus
10. So Please You, Sir, We Much Regret .... Yum-Yum, Pitti-Sing, Peep-Bo, Pooh-Bah, and Chorus
11. Were You Not to Ko-Ko Plighted .... Yum-Yum and Nanki-Poo
12. I am So Proud .... Ko-Ko, Pooh-Bah and Pish-Tush
13. Lots of Good Fib in the Sea .... Pitti-Sing and Chorus
14. The Hour of Gladness .... Katisha
15. Finale

ACT II

Musical Numbers

1. Braid the Raven Hair .... Pitti-Sing and Chorus
2. The Sun Whose Rays .... Yum-Yum
3. Madrigal: Brightly Dawns Our Wedding Day ... Yum-Yum, Pitti-Sing, Nanki-Poo, Pish-Tush
4. Here's a How-de-do .... Yum-Yum, Nanki-Poo, Ko-Ko
5. I'm the Emperor of Japan .... Mikado and Katisha
6. My Object All Sublime .... Mikado and Chorus
7. The Criminal Cried .... Pitti-Sing, Ko-Ko, Pooh-Bah and Chorus
8. Glee: See How the Fates Their Gifts Allot ...... Mikado, Katisha, Ko-Ko, Pitti-Sing, Pooh-Bah
9. The Flowers That Bloom in the Spring ... Nanki-Poo, and Ko-Ko
10. Alone and Yet Alive .... Katisha
11. Willow, Tit-Willow .... Ko-Ko
12. There is Beauty in the Bellow of the Blast ..... Katisha and Ko-Ko
13. Finale: For He's Gone and Married Yum-Yum.

With the Bloomfield College Choir, ca. 1935.

noon and I'd help them with their opera scores. When you had to memorize an opera, you needed either a record player or a human who could play these scores. That was one thing I could do for them and I kind of enjoyed it. Then we would often go out to eat together. There was no sense in their making a double trip if they didn't have to.

One of the things that seemed to go with this job—every other year I had to play for the graduation exercises of Bloomfield College and Seminary, down the street. They had it one year at the First Presbyterian in Bloomfield and another year at Westminster Presbyterian. Evidently, back in the 1890s, there had been a group of conservatives in Bloomfield that had money; they left the First Presbyterian Church because it was becoming too "modern" and founded Westminster Presbyterian Church. Of course, they had to get a bigger organ than they'd had before. They'd get these expensive soloists from New York. You see, they had all the dough, but they didn't want to listen to the modern theology. Of course, some years later, after I had left, the two churches merged again. There's no reason to have two big Presbyterian churches there, fighting with each other.

Anyway, there I was at Westminster. First Presbyterian had an older history. Westminster was founded in the late 1800s. They could get the kind of minister they wanted, and they wouldn't take anybody from Princeton Seminary—they'd be "too modern." Of course, they had good people. Our two folks from Union actually came out of the First Presbyterian. Everything was very friendly. It took me a while to figure out some of this background, but I was lucky in getting that job.

One year, when the Bloomfield Seminary graduation was held at Westminster, a student, Frederick Jenkins, suggested the college should hire me year-round. The president of the college was a retired Presbyterian minister and he decided to hire me for twenty-five dollars a month to direct a choir, teach a course in hymnology, and play for chapel at 9 a.m.

We had fifteen or twenty members in the college choir and among them were some great soloists. We put the college on the map because we traipsed around to many small churches putting on concerts. We could jam the choir into three cars and put on concerts for

Bloomfield College and Seminary.

small humble churches for no fee. Most of them had student ministers. They got a pretty good bargain, just paying five dollars a car for gas. I would play some organ pieces too. I didn't want to make more than one trip, so I learned what questions to ask—"Does it have two octaves of pedals?" The local organists were usually mad at me afterwards because I would make the organ sound better than they did.

I found a few other things to do while I was in Bloomfield. I took on the organ position at Temple Sharey Tefilo and did consulting for the music publications of the Presbyterian Board of Christian Education, which included helping them develop a primary hymnal and book of anthems for junior choirs. Another directing opportunity was the mixed chorus of the Shering Corporation in Bloomfield. I chaired choral festivals for the state Federation of Music Clubs, and for fun I played in the Bloomfield Symphony.

Roberta rides a Siberian donkey, after her talk on junior choirs at the AGO regional convention, Wilkes-Barre, Pennsylvania, June 1938. Carl Roth assists.

It was during this long period that I finished my Master of Sacred Music degree at Union Theological Seminary, in 1935, and then my doctor's degree in 1945. I also passed the AGO Choirmaster exam.

⌁ 9 ⌁

BERT

$\mathcal{A}$fter I began teaching at Bloomfield College, I became aware of a certain student, Jacob Gijsbert Wiersma, who lived down the street from the old, two-story house where I had my upstairs apartment. His family had arrived in the United States on the liner *Hamburg* on May 18, 1930. Bert, not relishing farm work as his father had, had enrolled in the high school academy at Bloomfield College. After graduation, he had remained in Bloomfield to attend the four-year college while living "on a shoestring."

Bert took care of my coal furnace and did other kind deeds for me. He had been convinced in early childhood that he couldn't sing, and so he was not in the college choir. If I had gotten hold of him at a more tender age, I could have trained him to sing, but by the time I was in the picture, I thought it best to just encourage him to appreciate good music.

Bert would often come upstairs to check on whether it was warm enough for me.

J. Gijsbert Wiersma, Bloomfield College and Seminary, ca. 1938.

57

455 Franklin Street, Bloomfield, New Jersey.

That is how we got acquainted. When his college graduation was nearing, we decided to get married—immediately following the graduation ceremony. We figured that all the right people would already be there. So I first played for graduation, and then went out and put on a white jacket and white hat. My friend from the Guilmant School, Lillian Mecherle McCord, took over on the organ. One of my church soloists, Pauline Pierce, sang my composition "The Greatest of These Is Love."

We had taken my car out to the maid of honor Mary Wells's house and locked it in the garage so that the Bloomfield College students couldn't do anything to it. Many of them knew ahead of time that we were planning to get married on the night of graduation, but the president of the college did not. He was a man who prided himself on knowing what was going on. When he finally found out that night about the wedding, he said, "I suppose there were the usual preliminaries?"

We had driven up to Pennsylvania a few days before the wedding so that I could meet Bert's parents. The family farm was located near the small town of Wind Gap, near Nazareth and the larger city of Bethlehem. It was no coincidence that they had settled in "Moravian territory." Bert's parents had met in South Africa. His mother, Clara Margarete Lincke, was originally from Germany but had gone to South Africa to care for her older sister, Lydia, who was convalescing there after childbirth. Bert's father, Jacob Tjisse Wiersma, was from Friesland, in the northern part of Holland, and had arrived in South Africa in 1895 to take care of a herd of cattle which had been transported by freighter from Holland to South Africa.

Bert's father was a friend of Clara's sister, Lydia, and her husband, and so through them Bert's parents met. They were married in 1907 at the Moravian Church in Elim, South Africa.

Jacob, who had been brought up in the Dutch Reform Church, joined the Moravian Church at this point and entered its mission service, and the new couple then served in two locations in what is now Tanzania. Four children, the oldest of whom died in infancy, were born in Africa. Following a second son, Tjisse Olfert, and a daughter, Dorothea, the youngest was a roly-poly son named Jacob Gijsbert, nick-named "Dicki" (meaning "Chubby") and later "Bert." He was born on June 21, 1913. It is interesting that Bert and I shared the same nickname—during my college years I

Wedding photo, May 18, 1939.

59

had also acquired the name "Bert." After our marriage, somehow we became known as "Bert and Bertie," and this lasted through the Bloomfield period. Dorothea, later known to me as Bert's sister "Dot," also came to attend Bloomfield College and was an enthusiastic member of my college choir. So, you see, I was connected with this family in various ways.

In 1914, while Bert's parents were on furlough in Friesland, Germany declared war, and it was decided that the family either could not or would not return to Africa. On August 3, the same day that war was declared, twins—a boy and a girl—were born, but only the girl, Margarete, nicknamed "Gretel," survived. She became known to me after our wedding as Bert's sister "Greta." It was Greta who, with her husband John Armstrong, often visited the cabin at Best View, adding artistic touches to its decoration through the years.

Wiersma family portrait, Picher, Mecklenburg province, Germany, 1929. Dorothea, second from left; Bert, fifth from left; Greta, seventh from left.

7

or: *2 jaar*

Valable pour:

Valid for:

Gültig für: *zwei Jahre*

Handteekening van den houder:
(Signature du porteur)
(Signature of the bearer)
(Unterschrift des Paszinhabers)

Gijsbert Wiersma.

Beglaubigt

Picher, d. 14. Januar 1930

Der Gemeindevorstand

Bert Wiersma's Dutch passport, 1930.

Bert, of all the Wiersma siblings (there were six), had been the one deemed most likely to pursue a vocation in the church.

So, after our marriage in 1939, Bert began attending the theological seminary at Drew University. But after two years he realized that preaching a sermon did not seem to be his cup of tea—in fact, putting sermons together was absolute torture. I always felt that you've got to like doing that sort of thing or you're in the wrong business. Bert decided to withdraw from the seminary and take a position as assistant to the director of the Y.M.C.A. in Newark. At around this time, my aunt Marenda arranged for Bert to take some aptitude tests in Boston. It was discovered that he had unusual mechanical aptitude and was interested in working with people. He was really very clever at inventing things. Later, when the field of occupational therapy opened up to him, he wondered why nobody had suggested this to him before.

Then, sometime after our daughter Grace was born, Bert received a notice to report to the U.S. Army induction office. I drove him to the induction center and had to leave him there. I didn't think they would take him because of his "bum back," but I soon got a call from him.

"Honey, I'm in. *Your friend Robinson didn't make it.*"

And here I'd thought Clarence Robinson was as healthy a person as anybody else.

During a training session in Monterey, California, just before he was to be shipped overseas, Bert sprained his ankle. He had always had a fear of high places. At this point in his Army training, he was told to "jump." Instead, he absolutely froze. Someone then pushed him over the precipice and a sprained ankle was the result. On account of this accident, Bert remained in the United States throughout the war. He served in three locations as an Army medic and later was able to tell lots of hair-raising stories about medical practice (or malpractice) on an Army post.

Arriving in each new place, Bert would call me in New Jersey and say, "Well, I'm in so-and-so. Who do you know here?" When he called from Denver, Colorado, I told him, "Go to the Episcopal cathedral and introduce yourself to David Pew." David had been a classmate of mine at Union Seminary, and despite having been known as a perpetual bachelor for quite some time, he had just recently married. I knew my classmates would all be anxious to hear any information I could pass on to them about the new Mrs. Pew. Bert looked them up within his first twenty-four hours in Denver. It happened that Mrs. Pew was the sort of person who kept on the lookout for servicemen at church, and when she realized that Bert was married to me, she said, "You wait right here, you're going home with us for dinner." From then on, Bert was like a member of their household.

Bert managed to live through his stint in the Army, and then got started in the field of occupational therapy when we moved to Buffalo. Thanks to the Army, he was able to attend Buffalo State College, doing graduate work in industrial arts and then an internship in occupational therapy at the Buffalo State Hospital. All this schooling was subsidized by Uncle Sam, because Bert had done his duty in the Army. When he started the OT internship, he said, "You know, honey, this is what I've been looking for all my life." And so OT became his specialty. Bert continued working at Buffalo State Hospital and even took a year off to get his professional qualification at Richmond Professional Institute in Richmond, Virginia.

When my job offer at Calvary Presbyterian Church in Riverside, California came in, Bert thought, "Oh boy! I'm sure I can get a job out there." In California, he did find good jobs in special schools for handicapped kids, and he took additional professional training at the University of Southern California in Pasadena. He continued in this field until he retired in 1975.

Amongst our friends, Bert was known for the saying: "If you want a good husband, marry a Dutchman." And I would certainly agree.

❧

GRACE

$\mathfrak{J}$t was a Dutch custom to name the first girl in a family for the maternal grandmother, and so when our baby girl arrived on October 4, 1942, she was named Grace Claire, combining the names of both our mothers. We proudly sent out musical birth announcements with Grace's part (the melody of "Rock-A-Bye Baby") at the top, the first two measures of "The Greatest of These Is Love" as my part in the middle, and one long, low note for Bert in the bass register.

Everybody said this was the cleverest birth announcement that they had seen.

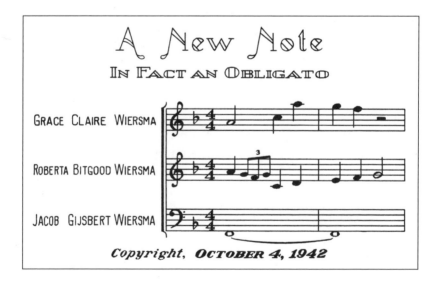

64

Grace was baptized before she was a year old, and for this occasion I wrote a chorale prelude based on the hymn tune "Jewels." Unfortunately while I was playing the piece, an usher called out loudly, "Would all of the mothers of the babies hold up your hands so we can give you each a rose?" Bert was there holding Grace and some people wondered about that poor man with the baby, and where her mother could be. Well, she was playing the organ!

Grace and Roberta at the console, Westminster Presbyterian Church, ca. 1945.

One of Grace's first words was "Army." She would say "aah-mee" in response to the question, "Where is your daddy?" While Bert was away, we lived through various crises including a coal shortage. We had run out of coal and couldn't get more, but there I was with a baby. Luckily, somebody from the college gave me a few wheelbarrows of coal to tide us over.

The summer before Grace was two, Bert came home on furlough. I was in New London playing for the summer at the Pequot Chapel. We had arranged it so that several organists in New Jersey would "gang up" and give each other a vacation and this was mine. I told Bert, "Grace is good in church—she can sit with you." But she proved me wrong. During the solo, Grace got away from Bert and came straight up the aisle. She pushed a chair over in order to crawl up onto the organ bench, got me around the neck with a stranglehold and said: "I love you, Mummy." Under my breath, I said, "You

Roberta and Grace, ca. 1952.

go and sit in that chair." Of course, everyone in the congregation enjoyed all this.

While Bert was in the service, I used to ask college boys to baby-sit so that Grace wouldn't forget what men looked like. Also, I didn't have to worry about boys walking home late at night. One of them was named Joe, and when Grace would wake up in the night, I would often hear a little voice saying, "Hey Joe." When she realized it was me, she would say, "Aw shucks, Mummy, I wanted Joe."

At age four, arriving late to nursery school, Grace reported to her teacher that she had just been to New York to hear the Brahms *Alto Rhapsody*. This had been a performance arranged by Dr. Clarence Dickinson as part of the morning chapel service at Union Theological Seminary. The singer was none other than Marian Anderson. The only way I could go was to take Grace, and so she was late for Miss Bleeker's school that day.

I pretty much let Grace roll with the punches and didn't try to keep her young. She was enrolled in various after-school activities in Buffalo including art, drama, piano lessons, and of course, junior choir. She occasionally sang solos and sometimes went along to an organ lesson. At age seven, she began to play the flute.

Grace remembers air-raid drills at her school in Buffalo. Later, when we moved to Riverside, California, there were no air-raid drills, but when she heard noisy planes, she dove under the bed anyway.

At age ten, Grace attended her first AGO convention in San Francisco, and she has been addicted to them ever since. Grace's first date actually occurred at the New York convention in 1956 and was the result of her losing a shoe under a pew. The young man behind her, Pete Daniels, who later took over the Moller Organ Company, retrieved it. At intermission, he asked my permission to take her to dinner.

Later on, Grace sometimes turned pages for me, including once at a recital I played on the big outdoor organ in San Diego's Balboa Park.

During her junior year of high school, a talent scout from a local community theatre group spotted Grace in a school production and thought she would make a perfect "Lotus Blossom" for an upcoming production of *Teahouse of the August Moon*. She auditioned and got the part. Rehearsals were every night from 7 to 10 p.m. Either Bert or I was there each night at 10 to pick her up before the adults went

"Lotus Blossom," 1958.

out to drink. When it came time for the performances, Grace was given a fancy black hairdo. She was perfect for the part. I always wondered if that got her interested in the Orient.

The night before Grace was to graduate from high school, I got the message from Calvary Presbyterian that I should look for a job elsewhere. This was a terrific blow. I just couldn't believe what I was hearing. I had been asked to meet with several members of the Session, without knowing the purpose. The spokesman had a speech all written out: "You offer us the finest music, the finest taste, and the finest technique, but this is not what Calvary Church needs right now. We know you're going to attend the AGO convention in Detroit this summer and we suggest you look there for another job."

I was apparently too highbrow for them.

Grace was scheduled to start her freshman year at San Francisco State College that fall. She and Bert drove across country to meet me in Detroit, where I had flown ahead to attend the convention and look into prospects for a new job. After a short vacation back east, we drove to Riverside via San Francisco. We found Grace a place to live in a large rooming house where one meal a day was served, and then we returned home to pack up. Bert later drove her up to college while I prepared to leave California. That Christmas, Grace flew to visit us in our new home in Detroit.

I seldom returned to California after that, but in 1987 I was invited to give a recital at Calvary Church, twenty-seven years after being dismissed. The occasion was the celebration of Calvary's centennial anniversary. Grace flew down from Berkeley, where she was then doing graduate work, to turn pages for me. We attended the Sunday morning service together, and I was asked to stand and be recognized. The recital was later on the same day, and the house was packed. Even Grace's former drama teacher came to the recital and reception. When I finished playing, the audience—composed partly of church people, and partly of musicians I had known in the area for years—went wild. I had to go out several times for a bow, and when I came back to the organ the last time, Grace said, "Look who's laughing now!"

By 1978, after two divorces and with her master's degree in Chinese, Grace was living and working in Hong Kong. Bert and I made the trip that year to visit her. We enjoyed most of our sightseeing in a rented car—Grace was afraid we'd expire from the heat, and an air-conditioned car was the solution. We even had a visit to McDonald's on the beach in Repulse Bay. Unfortunately, we lost several days to a typhoon. We were all supposed to take the one-hour ferry ride to the Portuguese colony of Macau and stay there overnight. Instead, Bert and I stayed hunkered down in our hotel room for twenty-four hours.

I traveled again later to see Grace, this time in Hawaii. The year was 1989 and I was to meet my new son-in-law, Stuart Kiang, whom Grace had met in Peking when she was there studying on a fellowship. It was fun spending two weeks bouncing from a condo in Waikiki to a mother-in-law apartment on the north shore of Oahu. The heat was a problem there, too, but Grace and I also flew to Maui, where we took a drive up the mountain to a cool volcanic crater and visited Brian Kelly from Michigan days, now living in Lahaina.

Dorothy Len Lau, Roberta and Grace, Honolulu, 1989.

Roberta and Frederick Swann at Central Union Church, Honolulu, 1989.

One memorable event was a crab fest at Grace and Stuart's place, complete with newspapers spread out on the table so that we could make a mess. Stuart's mother, Dorothy, and I hit it off well when we discovered that we both knew how to eat shellfish. I was glad to be able to play for her on the organ at Central Union Congregational Church in Honolulu, which was just across the street from Dorothy's apartment. I had known the organist there for years, and he graciously allowed me a "playing visit." Grace and I went back for the Sunday service, and you can imagine our surprise to find that Fred Swann was the visiting organist that week! After this visit, I had a nice note from Dorothy saying how much she appreciated Grace, who was like one of her own family.

Sometime during the next year, Grace phoned from Honolulu and said, "I'm getting my Ph.D.—are you coming?"

"Of course I'm coming."

I took two Sundays off and flew to the graduation ceremony in Berkeley. It was exciting and I'm only sorry that Bert wasn't there to see it. I'm afraid he thought it would never happen.

In Berkeley, Grace, Stuart, and I stayed at the home of Grace's friend Sondra, who was then out of town. The night of the graduation we went out for a nightcap with Grace's professor and came back to the house around midnight, only to discover that the key to this borrowed home had been misplaced. This made a memorable evening even more memorable, as we had to call a locksmith to help us get in. I shivered in the car while he did his work.

Now Grace is my "brain" and I'm happy to have somebody smart around. She takes me to all kinds of concerts and events. That kid of mine is funny—she keeps me cool on hot days with an ice pack.

I'm sad when I don't remember to thank people for the nice things they do for me, but Grace helps me keep track. She alphabetizes my incoming mail in a notebook where letters are preserved in plastic sleeves. Today a letter came from Andy Crocker Wheeler, who does a good job of keeping in touch with Connecticut College alumnae, and Grace has already put it into a plastic sleeve.

While I read my mail I'm listening to a recording of Moravian music which my son-in-law Stuart bought for me. It is nice to have such attentive kids. After living in Hong Kong for several years, Grace and Stuart are now living in the Boston area and I can see them frequently.

~ 11 ~

BUFFALO

I left Bloomfield in 1947, after fifteen years, because it was such a hard place to work with changes of ministers and so forth. Another job had landed in my lap. The secretary at Union Seminary called me and said, "There's a fine church opening in Buffalo. It's a Lutheran church. I think you'd like a Lutheran church—you like liturgy—and Dr. Ralph Loew, the pastor, is coming down. Now you understand—they've asked for a man." Oh, yes— they always do! "But I'm going to beg Dr. Loew to talk with you."

At the interview, Dr. Loew said, "Well, tell us about your teachers in New York!" So he had those well-known names—but in the meantime, a magazine article had just come out about me, and my "mug shot" was on the cover. The magazine was called *New Jersey Music*. Dr. Loew just happened to have come across this little magazine, and he was passing it around while doing all this talking.

One fellow sitting in the back said, "If you hire somebody like this, I'll double my pledge."

And they all said, "What is Charlie reading over there?"

It was just *New Jersey Music*, relating various of my accomplishments at a fairly early age.

"Ooh—well," they said, "OK, get her up here!"

Dr. Loew showed me all around the church, and I met everybody on the staff and met some of the committee folks. He said, "You know, we're due for a new organ here, and I think that probably you're the one to sell them the bill of goods." They had had an older organist there whose wife was a voice teacher, and her students would often come in and do solos for the service. "Maybe you can get some of the adults in the congregation who sing well to be in a choir." They did have an adult singing group, but some of the "old guys" in the church who liked those soloists didn't like this group to sing for the service. So Dr. Loew's idea was that if they hired somebody from the "outside," they would take over the existing adult group and make them the service choir. Then they'd still have their pick of good soloists if they wanted them. He begged me to start on Au-

Roberta Bitgood, ca. 1950.

gust 1, because of the awkward situation there. They didn't require much except Sunday mornings. At that point they didn't even have a substitute for Sunday mornings, so I said, "OK, I'll start August 1."

This was Holy Trinity Lutheran Church, 1080 Main Street, Buffalo, New York. At that time, Dr. Loew was already becoming prominent in the United Lutheran Church, and it was only a little bit after this, after I'd accepted the job, that he and his wife were suddenly on their way to Europe. This was in 1952, not long after the war. At that point I had realized that my boss was a big wheel, a fine preacher, an all-around person, and a pretty good pianist too. I think Ralph had done his share of organ playing when he was going through seminary.

I remember when we first arrived there—we stayed in a furnished room right across the street from the church—and it was hot. After a brief but uncomfortable period, we moved into an upstairs flat further from the church. When we returned home at night, we made Grace take off her shoes, because the neighbors complained to the

73

MUSIC CORNER

Hymn of the Month

During November we often concentrate on Hymns of Praise, as we approach the Thanksgiving season. In our book is a fine Hymn of English origin that we will do well to know— No. 487—"Praise, O Praise Our God and King". The words are set to verse by John Milton from Psalm 136. Sir Henry Baker used this hymn in "Hymns Ancient and Modern" which he published in 1861, and this has been the accepted Hymnal of the Anglican Church for many years. The tune Monkland first appeared in "Hymn Tunes of the United Brethren" which was published in 1824. This arrangement of the tune is by John Bernard Wilkes, who was an organist of superior ability born in 1785. This tune has much of the strong wholesome austerity typical of the English Hymn tunes of that period, and it should be easy to sing because of its limited range.

Mendelssohn's "Hymn of Praise"

On Sunday afternoon November 20 our Chancel Choir presents a favorite Thanksgiving work of major proportions, the "Hymn of Praise" by Mendelssohn. The composition is Mendelssohn at his best. It is dramatic and yet solid music. There is scarcely a conoisseur of choral literature that does not know this great work as the "Lobgesang". Unlike "Elijah" and "St. Paul" this work can be performed in an hour's time without cuts. Church performances of his longer oratorios must needs use many cuts. Originally this was of course written for orchestra and chorus, and at the beginning is a Sinfonia of some length which was originally intended as a long introduction to the work to set the mood and give out much of the thematic material to follow later in the choral section. This Sinfonia will be somewhat shortened for the organ introduction.

In discussing oratorios we often wonder what our favorite selections are in them. Certainly the best known section we find here is the duet, with chorus, "I Waited for the Lord", plus Mendelssohn's version of the great chorale "Now Thank We all Our God." A stirring theme in the first chorus is first given out by the male voices on the words "All that hath life and breath, sing to the Lord," and this is reiterated effectively at the very end of the last chorus. The soprano solo with women's chorus "Praise Thou the Lord, O My Spirit", an arrangement of Psalm 103, has been a great favorite with all who knew it. Many famous tenors have especially enjoyed "The Sorrows of Death" with its stirring theme of uncertainty on the words "Watchman, will the night soon pass?", answered by the soprano and full choir with full assurance: "The Night is Departing".

To our knowledge this will be the second performance in Buffalo, having been sung at the First Presbyterian Church once a few years ago. It is to be hoped that our congregation will come and bring their friends to hear this great Thanksgiving Music.

Our Church Paper

Published in the interest of the English Evangelical Lutheran Church of the Holy Trinity, Buffalo, N. Y.

Lutheran Church of the Holy Trinity
Main Street, above North Street
Phone, SU-2400

THE REV. RALPH W. LOEW, D.D.
Pastor
380 Parker Avenue
AM. 7206

THE REV. FRANKLIN L. JENSEN
Associate Pastor
96 Crescent Avenue
AM. 8992

DR. ROBERTA BITGOOD
Director of Music
197 Kettering Drive
UN. 5408

Foreign Missionaries
EMERITUS
REV. ERNST NEUDOERFFER, D.D.
Dean, Theological Seminary
Rajahmundry, India

THE REV. DONALD M. WILSON
Japan

Miss Alice Niederhauser..Office Secretary
SU. 2400

W. G. Stroman.........................Treasurer

James G. Wheaton.......................Sexton
69 Girard Place

"See the NEW Sunday Schedule"

landlord about the "patter of little feet." I didn't actually start rehearsing the choir seriously until the last week of August.

That job turned out to be a very happy situation—we got the first postwar organ in Buffalo, and it was a Moller. People began to sit up and take notice when I arrived. They sent me out to all sorts of places to look at organs, and said, "Spare no expense—don't take any money from the organ companies. You let us pay your way, and you go any place you want to."

Well, of course, I thought a Skinner would be great. But one of the accountants in the church had seen a report that Skinner was— even at that time—in bad financial straits. This man owned a lumber company and he would try to explain to me, "If my company is doing business with anybody that has as bad a credit rating as they do, I wouldn't do business with them, because at some time, it's going to catch up." So they didn't dare to do business with Skinner.

Then someone asked me, "Do you think that Moller cannot build an organ you'd be proud of?"

"I don't think that's fair for me to answer, because I know one or two Mollers I think are great, and I know I was brought up on one I hate."

So I went down to Maryland to visit the factory and talk to the VIPs, Riley Daniels and Ted Moller, the son of the original founder. I remember taking the sleeper to Hagerstown. We were sure we had maybe forty thousand dollars to spend. At that time forty thousand wasn't too bad. I saw three organs about the size we thought we could afford, which was a modest-sized three-manual instrument, and then I got the bright idea that if we got a bigger console, we could add a solo division later on.

I still hadn't realized that Ted Moller was a very close friend of our pastor and that they served on one of those Lutheran mission boards together. But they didn't use that to influence me. I had to be convinced that this was the thing to do. It was that trip to Hagerstown that did it. We could buy an organ the size of any of those three. There was one in very live acoustics and there was one in dead acoustics, because of the carpeting. They were all fairly sizable three-manuals and they all sounded good. Of course, as I said, I was brought

I'm gonna take whatever pitch & tempo I darn please—so wait for mama!

Drawing by Cliff Hehr

Cartoon by choir member Clifford Hehr.

up on an early Moller that I grew to dislike, right here in New London. But after trying some of those others, I said, "I'll be satisfied with a Moller."

The Moller representative started paying regular visits to Buffalo. The president, Ted Moller, even came up for the dedication. People said that he never went to organ dedications, but he was in Buffalo for that one. Since then, Holy Trinity has made huge additions to the organ. But I provided the fourth manual with nothing on it except couplers. I figured that if I had a great to solo 4-foot coupler, it could act like a solo once in a while.

I used children's choirs in the back balcony, and we had to have microphones and speakers up there so that the sound would be simultaneous. I taught two or three adult choir members how to help me by beating time so that we could be a mile away from each other and not get our signals mixed. One or two very fine children's voices fell into my lap. One boy had been at the Columbus Boy Choir School for a year or so—I think that his parents couldn't manage to send him back. There were actually three lovely little singers in that crowd. One little boy who was about nine had one of the biggest soprano voices I'd ever heard—he'd go right on up to the sky without thinking anything about it. That surely helped add quality to the children's choir.

In Buffalo we had to learn to cope with snowstorms. We had bought a house six miles from the church in a new subdivision. The first half mile into town was not usually plowed very early, so occasionally if I had an 8 a.m. Communion service, I would have Bert drive me to the church the night before, rather than worry all night that our slightly older car would not start in the morning. We were a one-car family then. I kept a studio couch at the church.

We lived in Buffalo five years. I sometimes think the worst thing I did was to leave there. But I had a job offer in California, from a minister I'd known at Westminster Church in New Jersey. Denton Gerow had been one of the assistant ministers who had been kicked around at that conservative church. He'd gotten to be something of a VIP there in California Presbyterian circles. It was Dr. Gerow who phoned from California.

I thought very reluctantly about moving, but with a husband who was dying to go back to California after having seen it in the Army, and being acquainted with the minister, it seemed like the right thing to do. We made an unforgettable trip across the country that summer with two of my organ students in the back seat with Grace. We went first to San Francisco to attend the AGO convention and then drove south to have a look at Riverside and make some decisions.

On moving day, our Hudson was really filled up. We started out late in the day, just to get out of town, but still had to make one last stop at the Green Stamp redemption center, to trade in our stamps for a pressure cooker. Many beef stews were cooked in that pressure cooker, first in California, then in Michigan, and finally here at Best View.

Grace was sad to leave behind her good friend Marilyn. By coincidence, Marilyn followed us from Buffalo to California one year later with her family.

&

$\sim$ 12 $\sim$

RIVERSIDE

Riverside was a fast-growing community. Calvary Presbyterian Church only had a parish hall, but was getting ready to build a new sanctuary. Again, I would be buying a new organ. They had told us Riverside was an ideal place to live: "... an hour from the mountains, an hour from the ocean, an hour from the desert, and an hour from the city."

Our first home there was fairly easy to move into as it was already furnished. The owners were going away to graduate school for one year and didn't want to let their house go, so we leased it. We arrived in October, and we were anxious to get Grace enrolled in fifth grade. That year gave us time to look for a home to buy. The one we finally decided on was a little closer to downtown and, although not quite so modern, it had more space. This was handy for having big choir parties. I remember that Bert and I threw a wedding anniversary party there before we had fully moved in.

My predecessor, Helge Pearson, was perhaps not the greatest technician, but he had been very well liked and was a hard act to follow. I inherited from him a responsibility for doing junior choir camps.

In that church they had four adult couples' clubs—different ages—because the meeting room wasn't big enough to accommodate all of them at once. There was one group for couples over fifty, one for those between forty and fifty, another for those between thirty and forty, and one for those between twenty and thirty. Each group would fill the place once a month. They always wanted some music—a community sing, or maybe a soloist.

A BACKWARD GLANCE FROM MY ORGAN LOFT

By Dr. Roberta Bitgood, Minister of Music,
Calvary Presbyterian Church, Riverside, California

What am I doing these days? I keep busy with workshops in church music, festivals and organ recitals, and the Guild conventions. The remainder of the time I devote to six choirs, the organ, the viola section of the Redlands University Community Symphony, civic projects — and of course I reserve some time for the nicest three fans a girl ever had: my husband, our teenage daughter, and Duke, our shaggy black mongrel, who, whenever he is let loose, heads straight for the organ loft at Calvary Church!

But I am ahead of myself. It was back in Connecticut where I was born, attended school and college, and plotted a career as violinist.

A Fiddler I Would Be!

Yes, it was violin that I studied seriously from the time I was five. I also picked out tunes on the piano, and in this I was aided and encouraged by my mother. But it was the violin that I chose to study at an early age. I played in school and church orchestras, participating in their outside engagements, too, which was good experience and helped me to gain facility.

Right here I must pause to admit that I was a naughty child about practicing violin. Instead, I doodled at the piano, exploring hymnals and piano materials borrowed from the public library. But this paid off in self-taught sight reading.

At age sixteen, when I went for my first formal piano lesson, I was able to sight-read fifth grade materials but unable to finger a C major scale correctly. It nearly drove my teacher mad!

The Organ Beckons

But again, I am getting ahead of myself. When I was a high school sophomore our Methodist Church bought a new organ. It fascinated me. I was eager to get my hands on it. But the church governing body did not look with favor on a young person toying with their new organ.

Here again I must pause ... to admit that I come from a long line of strong-minded women. So you can understand that I was not easily swayed from my determination to play our new organ. I found an ally in Mr. Howard Pierce, our math teacher, whose hobby was music. He consented to give me lessons on the organ at the church he served — and this opened a whole new world for me — the turning point of my life!

A few months later I got the opportunity to play my first service at Mr. Pierce's church. And soon after that my own church engaged me as assistant organist to play Sunday mornings — on that precious new organ! — and help direct the

Junior Choir. The job lasted all through my college years, and although it paid only $2.00 a week, it offered more of that good experience which is worth its weight in gold.

I Forsake The Fiddle

All my young life it had been planned that I would major in violin at Connecticut College. To make a long story short, I graduated with an *organ* major — perhaps the first person ever to major in organ at that institution. After graduation I landed a part time job at a New York settlement house as accompanist for dancing classes and clubs. I won a scholarship at Guilmant Organ School where I prepared for the Guild exams and passed the Associate exam after one year, the Fellowship the following year. While at Guilmant I had the very valuable experience of attending Sunday services guided by such skilled and dedicated church musicians as Clarence Dickinson, David McK. Williams and many others.

Continuing to work at part time jobs, I pursued my studies in New York at Teachers' College, Columbia; with a major in Music Education; two sessions of study at the School of Sacred Music of Union Theological Seminary; and private study with Dr. Dickinson and Dr. Williams.

My Organ Lofts

In later years I served at First Moravian Church, New York; First Presbyterian Church, New York; Westminster Prebyterian Church, Bloomfield, New Jersey; Bloomfield College and Seminary, Temple Sharey Tefilo, East Orange, New Jersey; Holy Trinity Lutheran Church, Buffalo, New York. The many wonderful friends introduced through these associations and through my activities with music workshops, festivals and organ recitals I count among the most satisfying rewards of my musical career.

And now, I have brought you right up to date on my career — to my organ loft at Calvary Presbyterian Church where Duke, our shaggy black mongrel, so loves to seclude himself.

Newsletter column written for Harold Flammer & Co., 1959.

I stayed at Calvary Presbyterian Church for eight years. The minister who was there when I arrived left after only two years. I always accused Denton of deserting me. I guess he was having a hard time for some reason, and I hadn't known this at first. But the man they brought in from northern California was also great. I had heard that at the Presbyterian church he'd served in Oakland, he wore a clerical collar and a cross. I wondered if he'd come to Riverside with that "rig" on, and so he did. He was well received. He'd had good music in Oakland, so I never worried about his taste. So it really was a shock at the end when I was fired. I'd been knocking myself out there for eight years.

That's one thing wrong with the Presbyterian form of government—the government "by the people." If you get a chairman of a worship committee who prefers hillbilly music, that person has too much authority.

I remember when I went home to tell Bert, I was thinking, "I don't dare tell you, but I've got to."

"They don't want me anymore."

"*What?*"

"I just got fired."

Bert put his arms around me for a long time, and Grace stood by silently while I sobbed. This must have been bewildering for her, too.

That summer, Bert and I discussed our various options. It occurred to me that we might just stay in California, but Bert was adamant, "I don't want to stay in any state where people would do this to you."

◡◠

~ 13 ~

FROM CALIFORNIA TO MICHIGAN

 remember that I had to do a workshop in Houston, Texas, and
from there I would go on to the Guild convention in Detroit.
Grace and Bert would follow a little later by car. I had flown to
Texas and flown on to Detroit. I had met Nellie Ebersole, who ran a
music program for the Detroit Council of Churches. She was a powerful lady and she made a lot of that particular job. She was in touch
not only with the big fancy churches but also with the humble little
ones, helping them with their leadership and developing conducting
classes. I think she'd been to one of those Christian practical training schools as well as to music school, and this was her thing, to work
through the Council of Churches.

I phoned Nellie—"Any jobs around? I'm looking."

She said, "Redford Presbyterian is looking for somebody, and Dr.
DeYoung has been in touch with me. Why don't I tell him you're in
town, and maybe you can go out there and see him."

So at the end of that convention I went out to Redford and
talked with Harry DeYoung a bit. He wanted the committee to meet
me. I was on my way to Connecticut for a vacation—Grace and Bert
had driven the car from California, and we were going on to New
York to visit his sister Greta. We did all the usual stuff in and around
New England, but in the meantime I concentrated on locating a job.
I stopped in at Union Seminary and I got a call from that Detroit
church while I was there. Would I be willing, on my way back to

California, to stop by and meet some of the choir?

"Yes, I'd be glad to."

So after our vacation we stopped in Detroit again. They put us up in a motel not far from the church, and I went over and met some of the committee. The musicians in the choir were very enthusiastic, thinking, "Oh, boy! If we get somebody like that, it will be just great!"

When I met with the committee people, they said, "Would you mind showing us how you work with some of our choir people?"

"Why not? Give me eight good singers—two on a part—and we'll do something."

So we spent twenty minutes rehearsing, and then we did a few things in the church. I thought this was about the most sensible audition I'd ever had, because, you know, you can work with people a little bit, and then they catch onto your signals.

Redford Church had a pretty good Schantz organ, which I liked, and they had two identical Sunday services—I was used to that—so once I felt it was "in the bag," then I could make up "my mind" what "we" were doing next.

Well, I had just finished writing my cantata *Joseph*, and we had done that on the last Sunday before I'd left Riverside for the convention. I knew I'd gotten fired, but I hadn't told any of the choir, for fear they wouldn't be able to sing. When I got back, I still wasn't planning to tell them right away. So there we were in San Francisco when one of my choir members bumped into me on the street. I said, "Oh! Do you want to ride back with us?"—because she was planning to take the bus back from San Francisco to Riverside. "Oh, ride back with us!"

By that time the choir in Riverside had heard the rumors, and they knew that I was coming back for the last time. But Shelley—I knew she didn't know, because otherwise she would have had something to say about it. I told Bert, "Don't say anything." Next morning—"Yes, I'll be there at choir"—she came to the rehearsal and when that processional came up the aisle and I realized Shelley wasn't there, I said, "Oh, somebody must have told Shelley." She was in the ladies' room weeping for an hour. You know, she'd had that long

Roberta Bitgood with massed choirs in the chancel of Calvary Presbyterian Church, Riverside.

ride with us and we hadn't let on. She had to find out another way.

All of a sudden it dawned on the church officials: "Why, they've got to sell the house; they've got to do this, that, and the other. We ought to give her a month of paid leave!"

Boy, they couldn't get rid of me fast enough!

"By golly," I said, "I'm going to give them the best music they've ever had this month, and they're going to have to sit there and take it, and I ain't leaving until the day after!"

I think the worst thing was when the kids found out that I was leaving—there was a circle of weeping children around at both postludes.

෴

_ᔕ 14 ᔭ_

DETROIT, BAY CITY,
AND BATTLE CREEK

Bert and I spent fifteen years in Michigan at a succession of three churches: Redford Presbyterian in Detroit, First Presbyterian in Bay City, and First Congregational in Battle Creek. The job at Redford Church was rather short-lived. There was a delicate political situation there, but the claim made by the minister was that I played too many pieces "in the minor." Looking back, I saw that I had played perhaps three pieces during Lent in minor keys. At least at that job I was given three months' severance pay. The first Sunday I wasn't there to play, the choir protested by coming into the service ten minutes late. I was relieved to be out of that situation, no doubt about it.

One can learn either humility or bitterness from such experiences. It was at this point that Bert and I considered joining the Peace Corps. If Bert's health had been better, we would probably have followed through on this.

Instead, we went to Bay City and stayed there for the next six years. "Rusty" Evans, who had also been director of music programs in the Bay City public schools, had been at First Presbyterian Church for forty or fifty years, so I had "big shoes" to fill. There had been one buffer person in between us, after Rusty's death, but he hadn't lasted.

The first stretch that I was there, I constantly heard, "Rusty did it this way, Rusty did it that way." It sounded like he was right up there next to God! It took a while to get over that feeling.

First Presbyterian had big children's choirs and that was my specialty. I had two wonderful helpers: Jean Nykamp, who directed the children's choirs from the balcony, and Nelda Taylor, who was a librarian.

Two of my high school organ students, Bob Sabourin and Jim Hill, went on to become very fine musicians. Later they both—in succession—landed the music position in the same church where they had once been my students. Jim is still there now.

After my stint in Bay City, I found it a pleasant surprise that I could still land a job like First Congregational in Battle Creek. I felt it was a very desirable job. They had a good program with graded choirs. Grace at some point invented the term "choirs from womb to tomb." The adult choir there was good and I would be following a series of people I admired, including Dan Byrens, my immediate predecessor.

I met many fine people and took part in a lot of "extracurriculars" while in Michigan. I served on the planning committee of the Michigan State University Church Music Workshops, led by Corliss Arnold; attended the University of Michigan Organ Seminars, organized by Marilyn Mason; continued to be involved in children's choir camps; and played my viola in the Saginaw and Battle Creek symphonies. The Choristers' Guild and Michigan Federated Music Clubs were often on my schedule too.

Roberta holds forth at Battle Creek choir dinner.

There were, of course, the usual recitals, organ dedications, and weddings. I remember playing for one wedding where the bride was thirty minutes late. The groom was having fits. There was nothing to do but keep on playing!

I took two trips to Europe during the years we were in Michigan. One trip was taken with Bert when he attended an international conference on occupational therapy in London. My most vivid memory of that trip is that when Bert said to me, "Honey, I'm getting tired of this Catholic business," I suggested he take a break and attend a Sunday morning worship service at the American Church in Paris. He took me up on the suggestion. Bert reported that there had been the usual American Protestant coffee hour afterward and that he had spoken to the organist. She inquired where I was. He replied, "Notre Dame." She confided that if she hadn't been working that's where she'd have been, too!

We enjoyed a lot of camaraderie with other church musicians in Michigan. I especially admired Calvert Shenk, who was then at the

Roberta models Bitgood sweatshirt at AGO national convention, Seattle, 1978.

Catholic church across the street from First Congregational in Battle Creek. I marveled at how many masses he played every week. The Southwestern Michigan Chapter of the AGO was up and running at that time and I offered whatever support and leadership I could. I did the same as a member of the Detroit chapter of Choristers' Guild and of Michigan Woman Composers.

There seemed to be a steady flow of colleagues coming to First Congregational to borrow this and that. One time, a fellow church musician, Ralph Deal, wanted to borrow the timpani—for his wedding, no less. My curiosity got the best of me and I had to show up to see just how he was going to make use of these things. I have to admit that the Purcell "Trumpet Voluntary" sounded just great with percussion in addition to brass!

David Graham, the associate minister at First Congregational while I was there, eventually became its senior clergy—this was a first in that church, I believe. And I was at First Congregational when I got the phone call about the AGO national presidency. There was a lot of hoopla, including a very gala farewell party when I retired, complete with a "Bach, Beethoven, Bitgood" sweatshirt. I left a lot of good friends and pleasant times behind—but many have stayed in touch.

_____ ᔓ 15 ᔕ _____

COMPOSITIONS

O nce, when I was a kid, my mother saw an ad in one of the
religious magazines that a new tune was being sought for
the text

> *I know not how that Bethlehem's babe could in the Godhead be;*
> *I only know that Jesus Christ has brought new life to me.*

I entered the contest and didn't win, but my tune got published
somewhere. I had been embarrassed that my mother had insisted on
submitting it, as I hadn't studied harmony yet. I didn't think it was
that good. But people used to think that if you could write notes on
paper, you were some kind of genius.

Sometime later, a hymn was sent to me for evaluation with the
text

> *Sound over all waters, reach out to all lands,*
> *The chorus of voices, the clasping of hands.*
> *Rise, hope of the nations, arise like the sun.*
> *All speech flows to music, all hearts beat as one.*

The existing tune had a 3/4 time signature and I felt that anything with that strong a text should be written in 4/4, so I wrote a new
setting. Later, I duplicated it myself to send out as a Christmas card.

My first bunch of pieces to be really published included "Rosa
Mystica." That was around 1935. H. W. Gray Company had a music

store on East 48th Street. The fellow behind the counter, John Holler, knew me by name. I had turned in some pieces and they were among others waiting to be reviewed in "the vault."

It happened that H. W. Gray himself attended a Guild dinner one night in New York. There was an empty chair beside me, and he came over and asked, "Young lady, do you mind if I sit here? I'm not an organist."

I answered, "Why, yes, Mr. Gray."

"How do you know my name?"

"Why wouldn't I know your name? Some of my best pieces are growing mold in your safe!"

BLOOMFIELD MUSICIAN'S COMPOSITION PUBLISHED

The H. W. Gray Company of New York has just released a sacred solo, "The Greatest of These," which was composed by Roberta Bitgood, organist and director of music at Westminster Presbyterian Church of Bloomfield. This solo is based on I Corinthians; 13. It has been sung many times here and elsewhere by Miss Pauline Pierce of the Westminster Church quartet, and other well-known singers. Three of Miss Bitgood's choral compositions were published in 1935 by the same company, and these have appeared on programs in many parts of the United States. The "Rosa Mystica," an unaccompanied Christmas carol for mixed voices, was sung in three of the large New York churches during the Christmas season.

He asked for my name and wrote it on the back of an old envelope. Shortly after that, he asked John Holler if there was anything written by me in the vault. Lo and behold! I started getting proofs the next week. Soon "Rosa Mystica" and several others of that period were in print.

The next time I saw John Holler, he said, "Kid, you've got it made. David McK. Williams just bought sixty copies of your piece 'Rosa Mystica,' and he's going to do it on Christmas Eve."

I was flabbergasted.

On Christmas Eve, after doing my usual duties, including a round of carol singing for shut-ins by the junior choir in Bloomfield, I took a 10 p.m. bus to get to St. Bartholomew's for the eleven o'clock service. I had to stand, as the seats were all gone, and remem-

Roberta and Agnes Armstrong with the "Ancient Alleluia" manuscript.

ber leaning against a pillar to hear my piece, done a lot more slowly than I had envisioned.

At some point thereafter, David McK. Williams commented to me, "Your music is so chaste, you must be the virgin of the virgins."

Some classmates overheard this and I acquired the nickname "Verge." Dr. Williams also used to address letters to me as "Dear Virgin." However, after I married Bert, he suddenly reverted to "Dear Roberta" whenever he wrote.

I remember sometimes being invited to have lunch out at H. W. Gray's summer place in Connecticut and I often met interesting people there. Mr. Gray's wife had died but he had a housekeeper who was a very good cook.

I was living in New Jersey when I wrote *Job*, and that was where it was first performed. I had a powerful bass soloist at that time who knew how to dramatize that text, and it was a good thing because he got more out of Satan's part than somebody else might have. The singers were reading from manuscript, but it was no more nerve-wracking than the average first performance. No one from H. W. Gray came out to hear it—none of them were particularly churchgoers. But they did publish the cantata.

"Give Me a Faith" has always been one of my best sellers. When I first took it to composition class, everybody laughed and said it was "corn."

"Stop laughing," I said, "I might make money on this piece!"

"Prayer Is the Soul's Sincere Desire," written in free rhythm, needs a real expert choir to sing it a capella. It is one of my favorites. I still can't stand the idea of it not being done a capella, so not all of my choirs have done it. Some of my music was written for a particular occasion—for instance, the "Chorale Prelude on Jewels," written for Grace's baptism.

My organ piece "On an Ancient Alleluia" was based on a chant set down in an old parchment manuscript that was brought to me from Europe by the parents of a Riverside choir member.

"Is this what you've been looking for?" they said.

My eyes got big as saucers because I knew it was several hundred years old. I could tell roughly how old because it was written on five lines rather than four, which would have been earlier. That old manuscript still hangs on my wall—I had glass put on both sides so that it could be reversed.

I've always been pleased to do commissioned works. My most recent commission was to write new settings for two hymn tunes. A certain Canon Van Dissel, located in South Australia, has just sent me the proofs and they will be copyrighted in the year 2000, published by GIA. It is good to still be productive.

"Poeme for Flute and Piano," composed ca. 1958, unpublished autograph.

21

4.

∽ 16 ∾

TEACHING

I've always said, "You have to have a good student in order to feel like a great teacher."

One of my first good students was Mary Elizabeth Compton. She was a teenager when I was first in New Jersey. She was a minister's daughter, one of three irrepressible sisters. Her mother was a typical minister's wife who did lots of things beyond the call of duty. Those girls were full of mischief, but Mary Elizabeth ended up at Juilliard, and then at Union Theological Seminary in the School of Sacred Music.

In Buffalo I had a fourteen-year-old student who "doodled" at the keyboard. He could play "Happy Birthday" in three keys at once, and because of this his mother thought he had promise. She was determined for him to have lessons. His parents both worked so I offered to go out to their house to give him lessons until he could find a piano teacher. Grace had to go along to the lessons sometimes. After a while, I suggested he take piano and organ on alternating weeks. When he was fifteen, he played in a competition held in Buffalo. The judges sat behind screens. I had convinced him to use the traditional touch instead of something of his own invention. He came in first. This student was Carl Staplin, who now teaches organ at Drake University.

Other students in Buffalo were Hans Vigeland, who was a brilliant adult student, Raymond Glover, who became an editor of the new Episcopal hymnal, and Mildred Fischle, who went on to get a doctorate and was a full-time school teacher in Buffalo. Mildred has had several good-sized church jobs, and she is still at it.

Ruth Storner Barrett worked in a doctor's office across the street from Holy Trinity in Buffalo and for convenience she would come over to practice there on her lunch hours. Once a week she took a lesson from me. She was a brilliant, fast learner.

At Calvary Presbyterian in Riverside, California, I had an older teenage student who was already an accomplished keyboard wizard. He came to his first lesson with unpublished pieces in hand. His first piece in print was "Christ Is Made the Sure Foundation." He had already had one rejection slip on it, and I encouraged him. "Ignore that letter," I told him. "They're crazy." It finally got published and became a best-seller overnight. Now Dale Wood has volumes in print, of course, and is a publisher himself.

I was at a Methodist junior choir camp in Michigan when the co-dean and accompanist for the camp "got up her nerve" and asked if she could study with me. I knew she was serious when she said, "What are you doing next Tuesday?" She was planning to enroll in a master's degree program at Western Michigan University and wanted to "brush up." I remember that she came to her second lesson with the youngest of her three children in tow and with one of the Franck chorales almost memorized. This student was none other than Julie Goodfellow, who has made so many long-distance trips to Best View to help me finish this book!

Bert and I were living at Best View by the time of Julie's master's recital, but we drove back to Michigan in order to attend. I just about burst my buttons, *Carl Staplin at the console of the Cathedral of St. Patrick, Norwich, Connecticut, May 1993.*

and so did Bert. This was one of only two times that I can recall being recognized at a recital for my teaching efforts.

Michael Noonan was an adorable fifteen-year-old boy when he stood by the organ watching me play the postludes at St. Mark's in Mystic, Connecticut. I asked Mike, "Wouldn't you like to learn to play?" His father had recently died and his mother had begun to work outside the home for the first time. I asked her if she could drive Mike to the church for organ lessons, and to practice there three times a week. She agreed to this and before long I felt he was ready to play for a service. When I needed to travel on Guild business, I asked the rector, "Are you willing for Mike to try his wings?" Of course, I sent Bert to see how Mike would do on Sunday. His comment later was, "Like a chip off the old block." I taught Mike for perhaps four years, and he later majored in music education and organ performance.

I think this watching for interest at the grass roots level is important. Leslie Spelman was a distinguished member of the Riverside–San Bernardino AGO chapter. I remember him telling me, "I make it a practice to always look for a teenager in my church to give a one-year scholarship to for organ study. Some of them take to it and some of them don't." Dr. Spelman would teach one kid for free for a year. I remember thinking, "Now that's a nice idea!" So later when Mike came to watch, I thought of this. I took him on, and he just went "Zoom!" This was all because someone thought to say to him, "Sit down and try it. It's fun!"

Sometimes students talk about having "trouble with the feet." I don't think the trouble is with the feet. I think the trouble is the coordination between brain, bass clef and pedal. Well, there was a period when I had to work with a physical therapist nearly every day. If somebody didn't see me for two or three days, they would remark, "Oh, your walking has really improved!" They would notice it, whereas I might not. So when somebody has trouble finding the right position for the left hand and the feet and the eye, I say to them, "Coordination between brain, bass clef and pedal!"

If everybody in the business could spare an hour a week for a scholarship student, this might help to ease the shortage of young organists. By the time somebody goes to college and enrolls in an organ department, they've already passed this stage. This may be a more low key way to start someone off than a week of Guild classes and organized activities, but it's certainly the way I got started. I have thought so often about Dr. Spelman looking for a teenager in his congregation each year. It was a kind of investment, because he had more than enough paying organ students at Redlands University.

Another thing I've done, when I had a whole string of choirs, is that I never rehearsed my kids for twenty minutes and sent them home. We always had the full hour. That way, when Christmas or Easter was coming up, there wouldn't be a longer rehearsal schedule to upset the parents. But during the last half-hour I would take them in to the organ. The kids would gather round, go through something they knew, and then they could take turns at the organ. "Well, now, do you want to play a bell today? All right, play it here. If you want to play a flute, you can play it here." Whether I actually got any organists out of that, I don't just know. But it was educational.

Speaking of education, I also think an organist should take the time and trouble to talk to the elementary music teachers in the area. When they want to organize a field trip, invite them to come and show their kids the organ. I'd give the teacher a list of the parts of the organ to review later, so that the kids might remember something

One organ, four hands—Julia Goodfellow and Roberta Bitgood in concert, ca. 1981.

the next time they were near an organ. Often during the visit I would remove the back of the console. You know, these were fourth, fifth, and sixth graders. They would be bussed in from the public school, and they were usually quite starry-eyed about it, because most of them would rarely hear anything but an electronic. Every once in a while I do see an article about somebody doing this. More people should do it. I had quite a few of those school visits in Battle Creek.

Another way to make friends for the organ is to find ways for young people to actually hear exciting organ music. Sometimes that's not easy if there's not a good organ around. In Battle Creek, we had the Kellogg Foundation and the Kellogg Junior High School. There was an auditorium that seated perhaps twenty-five hundred. It was used as a concert hall for community concerts and so on, and they had a big four-manual Aeolian-Skinner organ dating from about 1948. While it wasn't played an awful lot, once in a while the students would hear it played acceptably. They may not have had a classical recital on it too often, but even if you're playing in the pop style, a 1948 Aeolian-Skinner doesn't sound like a theatre organ. That was put in by Kellogg money—he thought it was important. And they kept it in pretty good repair.

I say, seize every opportunity to show off an organ: wedding rehearsals, before and after choir rehearsals, Sunday School. Be informative and enthusiastic. If you are not an advocate for your instrument, who will be? Open the door to the pipe chamber and let people see how it works. If there are problems with the organ, you can be candid, but it's important to keep your zeal for the pipe organ intact and express hope that the shortcomings will soon be corrected.

Teaching and educating folks about the organ has been a big part of my life. One of the nicest tributes I can recall was from a student who was actually a grandmother when she started studying with me. Here is what she wrote:

My Teacher

I heard you play, and
Your music thrilled my soul.
I asked you to teach me, and
You made me want to learn.

When I felt frustration,
Your kindness calmed me.
When all those black notes awed
Me, you quoted, "Any song can
Be learned if we practice it slowly enough."
When the melody lacked clarity, you cried,
"Lift those fingers high."

When I only "felt" my music, you prompted,
"Skill, rhythm, <u>then</u> heart."
When I erred in performance,
You comforted me with,
"We all make mistakes."

Today, someone said to me,
"Your music thrilled my soul.
Who is your teacher?"

I gave them your name.
I felt you would be proud.

—Arliss Benham

∞ 17 ∞

RETIREMENT

$\mathfrak{I}$ can say that I have pretty much enjoyed doing the same things since I retired to Best View that I did before. Here I completed two more terms as AGO president and got involved in the New London AGO chapter, which by the way was new since I had left the area long before. Two "retirement jobs," attending and giving recitals, traveling to AGO conventions, and swimming on a regular basis have kept me fully occupied. I still swim two or three times a week. Keeping in touch with friends is also important to me and I love letters and visitors. There were adjustments to be made after Bert died, of course, and recently I have faced some new changes in lifestyle—they've taken me "off the road," which means I do not simply jump in the car and go anymore without a driver. But I'm fortunate for all the good drivers I have found. Grace sees to it that everything is running smoothly around here.

My first retirement position was at St. Mark's Episcopal Church in Mystic. St. Mark's is an old church, built in 1865, and the organ is a 1957 Estey. There were two choirs, adult and youth, and two services on Sunday. At one point while I was there it was decided to rearrange the chancel, with the altar becoming a Communion table. This would have meant moving the organ console and the choir to the back of the sanctuary, leaving the pipes up front. I had some doubts about this, but in the end the change was not made until after I resigned.

I had only recently resigned from St. Mark's when Bert died in 1984, and it was important to me to play for his memorial service myself. The rector graciously accommodated me. There were a number of organists standing by that day in case I couldn't get through it, including my organ student Michael Noonan. My choir stood by, too, and practically raised the roof when they sang "For All the Saints" (SINE NOMINE)—I thought this was an appropriate hymn to do for Bert.

That same year I had run into trouble with losing the sensation in my feet. This was a strange thing to have happen—I noticed it on a Sunday morning at the organ. Eventually I had to learn how to walk again in the hospital. You might think this an impossible task for someone over seventy years of age, but as it happened I became friendly with another patient who was in the same situation. This was a young fellow in his twenties who had just lost a leg in an accident somehow. When I saw him clamber up and down those stairs in the PT department, I just figured that I could do it too.

At one point while I was out of commission, the rector asked me, "Have you thought about retiring for good?" I hadn't really thought about it; I figured that as long as I could play the Doxology with two feet, I would keep on playing, and that my condition was only tem-

At the console of the McNeely organ with the Chancel Choir, Crossroads Presbyterian Church, Waterford, Connecticut, ca. 1998. © 1999 Robert L. Bachman. Used by permission.

porary. But after that strong hint, I did actually resign. This was probably all for the best since Bert's final illness only came to light after I was out of the hospital.

Not long after Bert left us I had a call from Norma Branch, the organist of Waterford Presbyterian Church.

"Roberta, I've been wanting to get away and my husband has just bought tickets for the two of us to go to Europe. Wouldn't you know, we are supposed to leave on the day the new minister, John Webster, is being installed! How about taking over my job for six weeks?"

I knew Norma through the local music club and I also knew that Dr. John Webster was a graduate of Union Theological Seminary. So I thought, "Why not?" I ended up staying from 1984 until my official retirement on Easter Sunday, 1999.

The Waterford congregation was then using Harkness Chapel at Connecticut College as its place of worship. When they later built their own sanctuary, and renamed the church Crossroads Presbyterian, the question came up about an organ. I invited Alan McNeely, whom I'd known all his life, and who had been interested in organ pipes ever since he was ten years old, to attend the first meeting of the organ committee. He had experience working for the Austin Organ Company and I knew he had supervised the installation of a big four-manual organ for them. Alan was willing to work with us and to install an organ with no down payment, and not even a time schedule for payment. I've been very pleased with and proud of the instrument he built for us.

Around the time of my 90th birthday, I was given to understand that the organ was finally paid for, and at this time the church made a ceremony of dedicating the instrument to me. This made me stop and think. I believe the members of that church also appreciate the fine organ they now have, and wanted to express this concretely.

After I took the Crossroads job, the pain in my knees simply got worse and worse. Finally in 1988 I decided to go for broke and have both knees replaced at the same time. Usually people do one knee at a time, but one of my choir members, Dr. Stephen Heller, thought I might as well get it all over with at once. Grace was at that time doing her Ph.D. research in China, but she flew back to be here for the surgery. Dr. Heller was then on the staff of the Lawrence & Memorial Hospital in New London, and he kept very good track of me afterwards.

When it was time to try out my new knees, an 89-pound nurse came in and tried to get me up. She probably thought I was stubborn, but there was no way she could get me out of that rocker! Her eyes then got big as saucers when Dr. Heller and a big, strong male nurse he had recruited each got on one side of me and walked me down the hall. I only missed playing a couple of Sundays. On the way home from the hospital—Dr. Heller was transporting me—we stopped in at Harkness Chapel. I managed to climb the stairs down to the organ bench and played the Doxology straight through! So the surgery was successful. During the weeks that followed, Crossroads choir members took turns coming to the house with their own "meals on wheels." What a bunch!

Several of these choir members, including Shirley Alderson, Nancy Hare, and Madelyn Shafer, have continued to provide a helping hand from time to time, as has my Grace. In recent years, Grace has made more frequent visits here, and always would join the choir at rehearsal and on Sunday mornings. After the change of leadership

(Left) On the eve of knee replacement surgery, Harkness Chapel, Connecticut College, July 1988.
(Above) Dr. Stephen Heller and Roberta after a successful surgery.

105

ds, I quickly came to admire the Rev. Anne Fuhrmeister ╷ it was a pleasure to work with her right up to the end. was not easy for me. Now, since I no longer work with my ioir, I attend choir rehearsals elsewhere on Thursday nights, and ιnd it a pleasure to sing under my good friend John Anthony. It just doesn't seem right to be at home on that night of the week.

I have done quite a lot of travel in my retirement years, much of it connected with my AGO responsibilities. I made some trips back to places I'd worked previously, to give recitals and direct my own music. One of these occasions was the annual Music Sunday in Bay City when they did a Bitgood program at my old church. I enjoyed another trip to Europe in 1985, this time with Clara Pankow Miller—a longtime AGO pal from Buffalo days—to see some of the great historic organs. And there was the recital in 1987 at Calvary Church in Riverside—they had to open up the balcony to accommodate the crowd!

I still go to every AGO convention I can possibly get to. Seven or eight years ago I was ready to go out the door to a national convention in Texas, but something seemed to be wrong with my leg. I ended up going to the hospital instead, and put in another stint there to get over a case of cellulitis. More recently, I appreciated being honored at the 1998 national convention held in Denver, where I received the Guild's prestigious President's Award, now on display here in my home. Things like this are so unexpected, reminding me that

Joyce Jones and Roberta Bitgood, AGO regional convention, Worcester, Massachusetts, June 1999.

106

AGO President's Award, presented by Margaret M. Kemper, Denver, June 1998.

people are after all very thoughtful, and I wish that I could thank each one who had a hand in it.

Another real highlight of the last decade was what I like to call the "Bitgood Bash"—the Roberta Bitgood Jubilee put on in 1993 by my local AGO chapter. The chapter was then headed up by Marianna Wilcox and Mary Weber Hall. This was actually in honor of my 85th birthday. For one of the first times I can remember, I was truly speechless. I was just flabbergasted. (Well, I did recover enough to tell a few good stories at the closing dinner party!) I would never have expected such a thing to be organized here in New London. It was a real thrill to hear my former student Carl Staplin in recital at the Cathedral of St. Patrick in Norwich, and to hear the choral work I was commissioned to write, "Ye Works of the Lord," performed for the first time. To top it off, my cantata *Job* was also performed, along with a number of my other compositions, in Harkness Chapel. What a treat to see so many special friends, some of whom came from a considerable distance. This huge event ended with a hilarious human pipe organ performance—and I may say that there was plenty of hot air to power those pipes! My friend Corliss Arnold had writ-

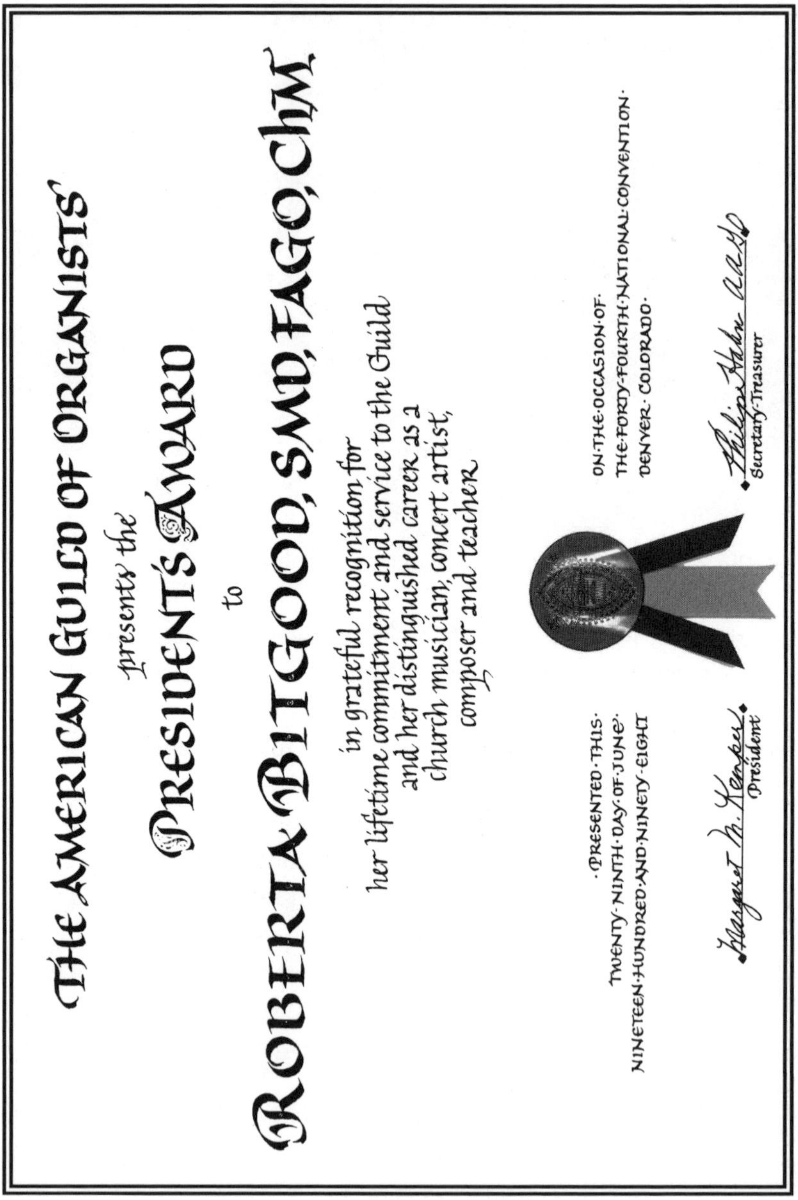

The American Guild of Organists'

presents the

President's Award

to

Roberta Bitgood, SMD, FAGO, ChM

in grateful recognition for
her lifetime commitment and service to the Guild
and her distinguished career as a
church musician, concert artist,
composer and teacher

·Presented·this·
twenty·ninth·day·of·june·
nineteen·hundred·and·ninety·eight

·on·the·occasion·of·
·the·forty·fourth·national·convention·
·denver·colorado·

August M. Harker
President

Philip Hahn, AAGO
Secretary-Treasurer

ten a new "Bitgood" text for Beethoven's "Ode to Joy," which was sung by quite a large group. This whole thing took a lot of effort and coordination. I felt thoroughly celebrated!

One other memorable event in recent years should be mentioned here. This was the "Bitgood Kids' Reunion," put together by a group of folks who had been members of my college choir at Bloomfield College and Seminary, way back in the thirties. We had a great time rehearsing on Sunday afternoon, and my Crossroads choir knocked themselves out once again, hosting the "Kids" at a potluck supper before the performance.

I have had some good tenants and helpers at Best View these last few years. Grace has kept my house up to snuff with various remodeling projects, including a new ramp entrance to help me come and go. One of my helpers, Marcus Perez, told me that he "had a girlfriend, who had a sister, who had a cat that needed a new home." So I was the happy recipient of FISBO, which really means "For Sale By Owner." This white cat is on my lap much of the time, and greets me whenever I come home from a recital or a swim. Some of my helpers have remained good friends long after moving on to other pursuits— "Fritz" is still a frequent visitor at Best View.

The "human pipe organ" accompanies the "Ode to Roberta," May 1993.

Greeting friends after Jubilee concert of Bitgood compositions.

John McCarthy, Roberta and Grace after the Jubilee recital by Carl Staplin.

Roberta and John Anthony, 1998. "Lobster is no laughing matter."

One thing I have neglected recently is string playing. I miss performing with the local college or semi-professional orchestra, something I have enjoyed in almost every place I've been. Of course, playing with the National Senior Symphony, organized here for several years by Victor Norman, was a great experience and provided a chance for me to dust off the viola. Unfortunately the Senior Symphony could not last forever. But various local senior centers and day care programs always seem to be looking for someone to play, so I still do some of that.

A few years ago, a canon from a small Anglican parish in South Australia wrote and asked me to contribute some hymn tune settings to a new book he was preparing. These are coming out soon, if I'm not mistaken, under the title *St. Francis Collection of Free Accompaniments to Hymn Tunes* (GIA Publications). For a while I had fun sending overnight express packets—what I called "e-mail"—from our little Quaker Hill post office all the way to South Australia, which as I learned was quite a remote place. Sometimes the Canon would telephone me from there, and I always enjoyed hearing that Australian accent at the other end of the line: "Helloow, this is Kurt Van Dissel!" And there are still more texts that I would like to set to music.

I remember a Cardinal Newman prayer that I stitched while visiting Bert at the Connecticut Hospice in Branford—maybe that should be my next composition project. That prayer was always a favorite of Aunt Marenda's. Just when Bert was so ill, I happened to find it printed up as an embroidery project. Bert's sister Greta, who spent much of that difficult period with us here, helped me find the right colors of thread to use.

> "Lord, support us all the day long, until the shadows lengthen and the evening comes, and the busy world is hushed, and the fever of life is over, and our work is done. Then in Thy mercy grant us a safe lodging and a holy rest, and peace at the last."

⌒

THE
ROBERTA
BITGOOD
JUBILEE

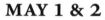

The
American
Guild of
Organists

New London
County Chapter

MAY 1 & 2
MCMXCIII

NORWICH AND NEW LONDON, CONNECTICUT

Carl Staplin, Organ

Saturday, May 1, 1993 • 7:30 p.m.

Cathedral of St. Patrick
NORWICH, CONNECTICUT

Works of Johann Sebastian Bach (1685-1750)

Passacaglia and Fugue in C Minor

Before Thy Throne I Now Appear (from the "Leipzig Collection")

Christ, Our Lord, to Jordan Came (from "Clavierübung, Part 3")

Fugue in E-flat Major (from "Clavierübung, Part 3")

Works of Roberta Bitgood (b. 1908)

Prelude on "Covenanters Tune" (1958)

Chorale Prelude on "God Himself Is With Us" (1953)

On An Ancient Alleluia (1962)

The 19th and 20th Century French School

Chorale in A Minor	César Franck (1822-1890)
Scherzo in E Major	Eugène Gigout (1844-1925)
God Among Us (from "La Nativité")	Olivier Messiaen (1908-1992)

You are cordially invited to greet the recitalist and Roberta Bitgood at a reception in the Cathedral Auditorium immediately following the program.

$\mathcal{A}$ Concert of Compositions of $\mathcal{R}$oberta $\mathcal{B}$itgood

Sunday, May 2, 1993 • 4:00 p.m.
HARKNESS CHAPEL • CONNECTICUT COLLEGE • NEW LONDON, CT

Give Me a Faith
Paul Althouse, Conductor; John Anthony, Organist;
Dale Tuller, Soprano; Carl Heinrich, Baritone

Meditation on "Kingsfold"
Eileen Hunt, AAGO, Organist

Be Still and Know that I am God
Mary Beth Lee, Soprano; Douglas Green, Organist

Wise Men Seeking Jesus
Mary Beth Lee, Soprano; Patricia Harper, Flutist; John Anthony, Organist

Ye Works of the Lord
An anthem commissioned especially for the Jubilee
Paul Althouse, Conductor; John Anthony, Organist

Choral Prelude on "Jewels"

Easter Morning in Holland (from Offertories from Afar)
Eileen Hunt, AAGO, Organist

The Greatest of These is Love
Mary Beth Lee, Soprano; Douglas Green, Organist

On an Ancient Alleluia
Eileen Hunt, AAGO, Organist

Introduction of Special Guests

Job
A Cantata for Mixed Voices
Paul L. Althouse, Conductor; John Anthony, Organist;
Job's Wife: Judy Barnard, Soprano; Job and The Lord: Roe Granger, Tenor;
Satan: Carl Heinrich, Baritone

The Combined Choirs are made up of members and friends of the New London County Chapter of the American Guild of Organists, and of members of various church choirs in New London County. Our chapter expresses appreciation to all who have sung or played instruments today and to all the choir directors who prepared the singers for the concert.

Gala Birthday Dinner
Sunday, May 2, 1993 • 6:30 p.m.

Blaustein Humanities Center
CONNECTICUT COLLEGE • New London, CONNECTICUT

Welcome
Marianna Wilcox, Dean, New London County Chapter, AGO

Invocation
The Rev. Dr. John Webster, Crossroads Presbyterian Church, Waterford, CT

Sung Grace: *God of All Lovely Sounds*
Bitgood

Introductions
Richard Bennett, ChM

Annual Meeting of the New London County Chapter, AGO

Prayer of Thanks
Rabbi Aaron Rosenberg, Temple Emanu-El, Waterford, CT

Presentations, Remarks, and Testimonials
Dr. Ronald Arnatt, FAGO, Past National President, AGO
Eileen Guenther, DMA, National Vice President, AGO
Eileen Hunt, AAGO, Region I Councillor

Response
Dr. Roberta Bitgood, FAGO, ChM

Closing Remarks and Benediction
The Rev. Dr. Walter Funk, Past National Chaplain, AGO, Princeton, NJ

Ode to Roberta
Dr. Corliss Arnold; *Ode to Joy*

Reminiscences
by
Friends & Colleagues

_____ ⧫ **18** ⧫ _____

BLOOMFIELD

Harry T. Taylor

Dr. Harry Taylor was a member of the Bloomfield College faculty from 1929 to 1965. His description of Roberta's contribution to the development of the college first appeared in his centennial history Bloomfield College, The First Century, 1868–1968, *published by Bloomfield College in 1970.*

When Roberta Bitgood came to Bloomfield she had just received the degree of Master of Sacred Music from Union Theological Seminary, and in 1945 was awarded her doctor's degree from the same institution. Miss Bitgood's anthems, sacred solos and organ pieces have been performed throughout the United States. One of her anthems, "The Greatest of These Is Love," is best known to Bloomfield students. She was a Fellow and Choirmaster of the American Guild of Organists and while at Bloomfield was organist and choir director at the Westminster Presbyterian Church.

Her accomplishments as director of music at Bloomfield leave untold the infelicitous circumstances under which she labored. With little resources in time and money (there was no music library, which made borrowing an art), a limited student body with modest talents and a schedule which became an appendage to the regular curriculum, the program achieved a remarkable discipline. It gained an eminence and influence not previously known. A person with engaging powers of persuasion and leadership, she captivated the imagination and loyalty of the students. Her contribution, even considering the unrecognized status of music, may truly be called an act of restoration.

Miss Bitgood's choirs in the first years consisted largely of male voices, which made the choice of music one of difficulty. But the advent of coeducation made possible such performances as Stainer's *Crucifixion*, and operettas such as *Trial by Jury*, *Pirates of Penzance*, and *The Mikado*, which were presented with gratifying results. President Hunter volunteered his compliments by stating to the directors that "the annual operetta given by our students under the direction of Miss Bitgood drew a capacity audience and was enthusiastically received."

Since the choir had become the institution's sole agent in the field of public relations, perhaps its most significant contribution was its visits to the alumni churches. These "pastoral calls" were most helpful in sustaining the interest of the churches in the work of Bloomfield. The concerts of sacred music brought splendid programs to communities which lacked resources to offer their own. Miss Bitgood made a four-part arrangement of the alma mater hymn, "Lux in Tenebris," which was sung at all concerts.

Perhaps through no other channel of communication, other than by its own graduates (who were deeply appreciative of these visits), did the communities of New Jersey learn about Bloomfield. The choir voluntarily represented the institution with a high degree of dedication. Miss Bitgood, unquestionably, made music a "serious subject" on the campus and brought to it a standard of excellence, for which the school and those who participated in this "excellence" owe her a debt of gratitude.

Robert Derick

*A retired church musician, Bob Derick teaches adult education in Riverside,
California, and does volunteer work in retirement homes, where he plays
piano, sings songs, and tells "clean stories." He played in the orchestra of
the Riverside Opera Company with Roberta and has been associated
with her in many other capacities as well.*

I've known Roberta since the thirties, when she was organist and choirmaster at Westminster Presbyterian Church in Bloomfield, New Jersey. At that time I was staying with the family of the baritone in the quartet at Westminster Presbyterian. We were in the Bloomfield–Glen Ridge area. Glen Ridge was quite elegant in those days.

On one occasion, my baritone friend was to be soloist for a private concert Mrs. H.H.A. Beach was to play in Glen Ridge. Well, he mentioned it to Roberta and she was most desirous of attending and meeting Mrs. Beach. So my friend the baritone, a William Ryder, snagged an invitation for her. I remember she wore some outfit with a bright red ribbon bow.

I mentioned the event to the girl I was dating and would later marry. Her sister, Dorothy Westra, was in the School of Sacred Music at Union Theological Seminary and was friendly with Roberta. My girlfriend and wife-to-be, Winifred Westra, sang often for Roberta because she was near Westminster and could be at the church in a matter of minutes. Later, Wynn (my wife) was a soloist for Roberta in the Jewish temple in East Orange, New Jersey. Our paths crossed often in that busy area.

Most important for us, Winifred Westra and Robert Derick were married in Roberta's church—Westminster Presbyterian—in 1938. No, Roberta did not play for the wedding because she was busy somewhere, and a friend of mine filled in.

Then children came along to our two families—Roberta's Grace and our Michael Christopher. I remember I was once assigned to take the two kids to the Bamberger Thanksgiving parade in New Jersey, a knock-off of the big Macy's parade in New York. My son Chris, about the same age as his companion that day but very much bigger, was not pleased that at the parade I held little Grace on my shoulder in order for her to be able to see the parade. Chris had to stand. He was tall enough and could see, of course, but he wasn't happy and I finally realized that all the little squeaks I was hearing from Grace were from moments when he had pinched her because I was leaving him out and he was jealous.

I also remember going with Roberta and Grace to an AGO meeting in Elizabeth, New Jersey. Nobody was pinched on that outing.

AGO events brought us together, and from time to time I'd play the Odell organ in Westminster, which had all the stop tabs in reverse. When they were up, the stops were *on*, but when down, *off*. Roberta eventually did get them changed before she left the church. But I can remember going there with my mind all turned around before discovering, with a little practice, that I could register as a normal organist likes to do.

As it turned out, we both were offered positions—almost at the same time—away from the New York metropolitan area. I went to Riverside, California, and Roberta to Buffalo.

(Bob Derick's reminiscence continues in Chapter 20)

Rev. William S. Ackerman

William Ackerman recently retired a second time after serving for fifteen years as part-time Minister of Visitation at the Presbyterian church of Toms River, following a thirty-three-year pastorate at the Presbyterian church of Livingston, New Jersey.

I entered Princeton Theological Seminary in September 1934 as a student for the Presbyterian ministry. My professor of speech, Dr. Donald Wheeler, soon discovered that I needed to improve my speaking voice and suggested that I learn better projection. My aunt, Julie B. Roubaud, a choir member at Westminster Presbyterian Church in Bloomfield, New Jersey, asked Roberta Bitgood, her choir director, if she would give me some voice lessons. I recall going to

Roberta's apartment for a period of time when she helped me with voice exercises. I have valued greatly what I gained from those lessons seventy-five years ago!

In 1993, my wife Dottie and I were privileged to attend the Roberta Bitgood Jubilee in New London, Connecticut. What a wonderful occasion to renew our friendship with Roberta and to celebrate such a musical giant!

Margaret (Williams) Mealy

Following her choir experience at Westminster Presbyterian in Bloomfield, New Jersey, Margaret Williams continued her study of music at Wellesley and Harvard and has been teaching music ever since. In addition to easy hymn harmonizations, she published Sing For Joy *with her husband, the Rev. Dr. Norman Mealy.*

My memories of Roberta at Westminster Church in Bloomfield, New Jersey, are enveloped in the sound of fine music pouring out of the organ loft all through my formative years. And down in the pews there was that sense of high esteem with which my parents and other adults spoke of "our organist."

A more personal memory is of us eight-year-old choristers dissolved in giggles, eyed tolerantly by "Miss Bitgood" while she continued firmly with rehearsing the anthem. In my high school years she flattered my growing musical skills by asking me to substitute for her at Wednesday prayer meetings and made me a very grown up tribute (as if to a colleague) by inscribing an *Oxford Book of Carols* with the words "To Margaret Williams with sincere appreciation of your many kindnesses to me."

And now I offer my sincere appreciation of her kind encouragement to me over the years and her continuing friendship, with all those musical overtones.

❦

$\backsim$ **19** $\backsim$

BUFFALO

Clara Pankow Miller

Clara Miller is the organist at the Christian Science Church in Poughkeepsie, New York. She has been a church musician for more than seventy-five years, and was one of the first to welcome Roberta to Buffalo.

When I first met Roberta, I lived on Grand Island. The Wiersma family used to come there to swim. Grace would usually stay up at the house with me so that Bert and Roberta could get some real exercise.

We stayed in touch even after I moved to River Forest, Illinois, and of course before long the Wiersmas had moved too.

In 1985, I called Roberta and suggested that we go on an organ tour of Europe together. I was delighted that she took me up on my suggestion, and she even adopted my idea of taking along a folding cane. All went well, except for the tour guide's habit of calling Roberta "Rebecca."

In each location the group we were with was asked if anyone wanted to play the organ. Roberta never missed an opportunity. We attended everything; in fact, we even took in some additional things that were not on the tour. There was a concert in Strassbourg that lasted until midnight, and in Dresden we took in a 6 a.m. mass all by ourselves. We also attended a wedding and a funeral in Freibourg.

There was political friction at every border and our bus was frequently searched. Roberta carried her word-scramble books everywhere we went, so she always had something to do if there was a

124

delay. I recall her saying, "You don't have to have brains to do these." She got me hooked on them and I've been doing them ever since.

Rev. Calder Gibson II

Calder Gibson retired in 1997 and is the current Hospice chaplain in Nelson County, Kentucky. He was an organ student of Roberta's in Buffalo and also head acolyte at Holy Trinity Lutheran Church during her tenure there.

"Watch Mama!"

Not the usual directions to issue from a choir director's mouth! It was the first rehearsal of the newly formed youth choir of Holy Trinity Lutheran Church in Buffalo, New York. The church had just brought on board its new organist and choir director—a.k.a. Minister of Music Roberta Bitgood FAGO (which translated, as we quickly learned, into Fellow of the American Guild of Organists). She joked easily with the dozen zit-faced adolescents, pointing out that we should never employ the prefix "not" before her last name, as in "Not-a-bit good." With such initial humor she easily won our attention and admiration. In fact, we not only learned she was good; she was excellent. And not only with the members of the senior and youth choirs. One of her greatest gifts was in seducing music out of that old clunker of an organ she had inherited from her predecessor, Lester Cherry. (Often I had to prop a pencil under a particular stop to keep it engaged.) And when the new four-manual Moller from Hagerstown, Maryland, was in place, Roberta became a veritable octopus. A cartoon sketched by an adult choir member depicted her as just that—a marine creature at the console. One tentacle kept her black beanie in place on her head, another turned the delicate page of French organ music, yet another adjusted a set of pistons, while still another selected several stops at once. Truly an "organic octopus!"

Just as quickly as we had learned to focus our eyes directly on Roberta rather than on the printed page when she snapped "Watch Mama!", we also discovered she was death on such teenage delights as chewing gum or dangling earrings on the fairer sex. She tried to

125

break choir members of their habit of keeping time with choir fold-ers, employing them as metronomes. Roberta was defeated, however, when it came to the bouncing bosoms of some of the heftier mem-bers of the adult choir, who in essence became the rhythm section of the chancel choir.

Church wasn't the only setting in which I got to know Roberta, Bert, and their daughter Grace. Serving as head acolyte at Holy Trin-ity, I needed to be at every service. Since Roberta did as well, it was only natural that I would accept their kind offer of a ride from the same Buffalo suburb to the downtown area where Holy Trinity is perched on the edge of the moraine left by the last glacier. Early Sun-day morning traffic was negligible as we plotted a straight route down to 1080 Main Street with the car radio furnishing background muzak while we chattered away.

One Sunday, as we half-listened, the announcer made a real boo-boo. He was supposed to say, "This program has been brought to you from the Buffalo City Mission." What all four of us distinctly heard, however, was the conversation stopper: "This program ... from the Buffalo Shitty Mission." From then on each Sunday, we listened with rapt attention to that particular promo. Alas, no repeats!

Roberta was a liberated woman long before Bella Abzug hit the scene. Sometimes I would be invited to the Wiersma residence for lunch or dinner. All meals there were communal in nature. Everyone pitched in, including Grace and myself, as well as anyone else pres-ent. (By contrast, in our "Leave it to Beaver" family, Mom always prepared the food, set the table, and cleared up the debris afterward.) Frequently Bert concocted the salad, I peeled the carrots and pota-toes, Roberta fried the hamburgers, and Grace set the table. Defin-itely a group grope!

Mentioning food, one single solitary grape became the source of much merriment between Roberta and myself. In the fall of 1950 I went off to college. It was Thanksgiving before I returned home. Leaning on the organ console to chat with Roberta, I noticed a dark object hiding under an adjacent choir pew. As I went to remove it, I was reprimanded by "Dr. B."

"It's a grape," she explained, stifling a giggle. "Or was a grape, now a raisin. Rolled off the Harvest Home decorations near the altar early in October … Jim missed it during his weekly cleanup … Eyes not as sharp as they used to be."

The raisin was still there at Christmas. By Easter it had vanished. Roberta explained it had gathered such dust swirls that even she couldn't stand it any longer and sent it on to raisin heaven. There ought to be an anthem there somewhere!

With Roberta as organist and choirmaster the pace of musical activities picked up at Holy Trinity. Visiting choirs and soloists appeared in our church, and we were proud to share works such as Roberta's cantata *Job* and her hauntingly beautiful Advent anthem "Rosa Mystica" with parishes of the greater Buffalo area. Symphony musicians would play at Holy Trinity, as did the entire Buffalo Philharmonic on occasion. This meant that cantatas of the "Greats" could be regularly performed—works by Bach, Handel, DuBois, etc. Often I turned pages for Roberta during such performances, as well as each Easter when Dr. B would perform Widor's Toccata as the postlude. Just as often, the edge of the brittle pages would crumble in my hands and I would have to fumble to get the proper page in front of the maestro's eyes.

Some organ concerts were more memorable than others, especially to a hormone-driven chief acolyte. At Roberta's request, I once turned pages for Claire Coci, a brilliant virtuoso who was also very easy on the eyes. Like the clergy, choir, and acolytes at Holy Trinity during that era, Roberta was accustomed to wearing the traditional black cassock and white cotta. In striking contrast that evening, Dr. Coci appeared on the organ bench in a white lace gown with very low décolletage that left nothing to the imagination. Her first act was to sweep the ankle-length frock back to the far end of the bench, pull her cream satin slip above her knees—and then pounce on the keys with firm fingers. My only salvation during the ninety-minute performance was to fix my eyes firmly on the notes of the music and *not* on the musician!

Years later when I was a mission developer on the south fork of eastern Long Island, my family and I accepted Roberta's invitation to spend a few days at her Shangri-la near New London, Connecticut. Her ingenuity was at its most creative when it came to accommodations. After a day of canoeing and a mouth-watering New England dinner, it came time for our two young sons to turn in. The boys had already scouted out the petite bed reserved for Dad and Mommie. Now the question was—where were they to sleep? Overhearing their inquiry, Roberta swept into the bedroom, opened two drawers in an adjacent dresser, emptied their contents, replaced the shelf paper with soft summer blankets, and motioned Calder III and Michael to test their new bunk beds. Quickly and with glee they responded to this novel invitation.

Roberta duly accepted our return invitation. My wife Bobbie, a very gracious Southern hostess and gourmet chef, set her usual sparkling table. Crystal glasses glittered, silver shimmered. Gold-band china plates and cut flowers denoted a command performance. Sweet Suffolk County corn plus famed Long Island potatoes were on the menu. I had spent a considerable sum at Gozman's Dock in Montauk for straight-from-the-sea lobsters. Roberta cast one glance at the finery and decreed a change in venue: "No way! We can't eat lobster like this!" So we consumed our feast on the dining room floor of the parsonage, a newspaper serving as our tablecloth, legs spread wide apart, with butter for the corn and lobster splattered on the diners as well as on the floor. Long after everyone else had finished, Roberta was still sucking the succulent meat from every crevice of her denizen from the deep. "The only way to eat lobster!" purred a satisfied Roberta.

Clifford N. Hehr

*Clifford Hehr was an art director and partner in a design firm,
from which he retired in 1991. The firm's projects were varied,
with emphasis on exhibit and graphic design.*

In November 1949, I became a member of Holy Trinity Lutheran
Church in Buffalo. I had attended services for some time, and been
greatly impressed not only by Dr. Ralph Loew's sermons but by the
quality of the music. Having had some choral experience, I decided
to join Holy Trinity's chancel choir. Of course, I had attended Dr.
Bitgood's recitals and realized she was an accomplished composer,
but I had never met her.

I expected the first rehearsal to be somewhat formidable. How
wrong I was! After a fairly painless audition, "Dr. B" declared me a
tenor, even though I had always been more comfortable as a baritone.
I suspect she was more in need of tenors than basses at that moment.
The first anthem I recall participating in was Mendelssohn's "There
Shall a Star," and it's been one of my favorites through the years.

Roberta had that endearing combination of serious motivation
and down-to-earth accessibility, all rolled into one charming personality. No matter how daunting the music, she managed to pull it out
of us, and always with good-natured skill.

As a designer, I sometimes try to capture on paper vignettes of
those who have made a special imprint on my life. So it was that,
after Roberta left for California, I came to draw a little collection of
"inside jokes" shared between RB and the choir. I recall quietly cir-
culating this booklet among choir members gathered one evening to
honor Roberta, who had returned to Buffalo for some event. The
reaction was more than I bargained for! From time to time, RB has
mentioned preserving this little memento—which must be in tatters
by now. Knowing she treasures this makes me especially proud to
have known her.

Carl B. Staplin

Dr. Carl Staplin AAGO *is Professor of Organ and Church Music
and Head of the Keyboard Area at Drake University. He is also
Minister of Music at First Christian Church in Des Moines, Iowa.*

I have always been blessed by having wonderful organ teachers.
My first recollection of Roberta (she was "Dr. B" to me) was in
Buffalo when I wanted to take pipe organ lessons as a teenager. I had
always loved the organ, and my mother had a close friend who told
about this wonderful new organist that had just been hired by Holy
Trinity Lutheran Church. I wanted to begin organ, and not continue my piano lessons, but Roberta wouldn't hear of it—she insisted
that I continue piano, and until I found another teacher she taught
me herself. I have always thanked her for insisting on that, because
at the time I didn't fully appreciate the importance of piano for an
organist.

Many activities in addition to my private lessons followed: various choral and organ programs she did at Holy Trinity, including the
dedication of the new Moller pipe organ, her chairing of the 1950
Buffalo AGO regional convention when her cantata *Job* was performed at her church, and performance classes with her group of private students, young and old.

I especially remember the trip with her family to San Francisco
for the 1952 national AGO convention. She had just accepted the
position at Calvary Presbyterian Church in Riverside and wanted to
see the situation beforehand. She was also to be a judge for the first
national AGO Young Organists Competition during the convention. Two of Roberta's students, Mildred Fischle and I, crossed the
U.S. with Roberta, Bert, and Grace in a big new Hudson. There are
many memories of that trip, and the convention made a lifelong
impression upon me as a young organist. I was just about to go off to
Syracuse University the following fall to study with Arthur Poister.

Another personal memory that comes to mind was after Roberta
took the position at Redford Presbyterian Church in Detroit. During

the years she was in California I didn't have an opportunity to see her, of course, since I was in the East. About 1962 I was teaching at Evansville College, and the college choir was invited to present a concert at Roberta's church. H. W. Gray had just published her piece "On an Ancient Alleluia" shortly before that. She also made a trip to Evansville while I was there to do a recital.

After I accepted a position at Drake University in Des Moines, Iowa, I invited Roberta, who by that time was national president of the AGO, to come and speak to the Central Iowa AGO chapter. I also saw her at the 1968 national AGO convention in Denver when Kathleen Thomerson and I did a two-organ recital for the convention. Roberta somehow managed to attend every national AGO convention and we always got "caught up" on those occasions.

During 1991, when I was doing research at Yale University, I made my first trip to Roberta's family home in Quaker Hill, Connecticut. She was still very active in her church position, directing and playing, and I remember going over to her church where she proudly showed me the pipe organ she had personally managed to have built for the church.

In 1993, I was deeply honored to be asked to play an organ recital in Connecticut for Roberta's 85th birthday celebration. That was a wonderful weekend, and so many of Roberta's friends were able to come from all over the country.

Most recently, my wife Phyllis and I were with Roberta and Grace for the 1998 AGO national convention in Denver.

The things I remember most about Dr. B were her many kindnesses to a young, teenage musician who idolized her. She had the patience of Job (not by accident!) in dealing with my youthful immaturity, and I shall always be grateful to her for her insistence on the best in everything, whether it was in music or in dealing with other people. There was a very spiritual attitude present in everything she did. She always went out of her way to help everyone—young and old. At the same time, she expected a serious musical commitment from anyone who studied with her. Still, her comments were always couched in kind words.

Thank you, Roberta, for all you did to encourage me as a young musician.

Mildred Fischle

Mildred Fischle is a college professor and church musician. She is currently director of music at St. Stephens/Bethlehem United Church of Christ and also serves on the board of the United Church Home in Buffalo.

It is very difficult to put in words my feelings for someone who has played such a significant role in my musical activities over many years. The words that come to mind include *mentor, teacher, friend, supporter,* and certainly the words *inspiration, respect,* and *love.*

One of my favorite memories is of the cross-country drive that I went on with Roberta, Bert, Grace, and Carl Staplin in order to attend the AGO convention in San Francisco. On that trip, we had a gray metal refrigerator from which we ate most of our meals. At times we would eat in a restaurant and learn even more about individuals' food preferences—other than cold cuts and the like. But what fun it was!

San Francisco was a wonderful time, going from recital to recital. Roberta *never* missed a recital. But one day, I had had my fill and took off for Chinatown.

From San Francisco we headed south only to have the universal joint of the car give out in Santa Monica. Then it was on to Riverside and Redlands.

We stayed in adequate motels, and some were better than others. I do remember one in, I believe, Reno where the shades had not been dusted in many a day, and Bert, who called me Myrtle, wrote in the dust, "Myrtle Slept Here."

If it were not for Roberta, I probably would never have gone to so many AGO conventions. My first one was in Boston. Virgil Fox was there with his black cape and red socks. I purchased a ukelele in Boston and on the train coming home Roberta entertained us by strumming the uke. Is there anything in music she can't do?

How fortunate we've been to have a person like Roberta in our lives. Her anthem "Give Me a Faith" gave me strength when my world was falling apart. She cared about her students and cared how they were treated in the churches. She has always been concerned for the smaller church as well as the larger, and has had a great impact on the music used in worship in the churches of western New York. I only wish some of the younger organists today could be so fortunate as to have a teacher and the example of someone like Roberta. She understood audiences and took them from where they were to know the best in music. I have had three excellent organ teachers in my lifetime, but it was Roberta who prepared me for serving churches both large and small.

Roberta, or as I have always called you, Dr. Bitgood, thank you, you're the best.

RIVERSIDE

Janet (Lynes) Gall

Janet Lynes was teaching first grade when Roberta came to Riverside to direct her church choir. She met her husband, Richard Gall, in Roberta's choir in 1955, and they were married a year later. She and her husband have continued to sing in church choirs for more than 40 years.

In September 1952, Dr. Roberta Bitgood came to Calvary Presbyterian Church in Riverside, California, from Holy Trinity Lutheran Church in Buffalo, New York. Dr. Denton Gerow felt that music was very important, and when our former choir director left to return to college to become a teacher, Dr. Gerow turned to his friend of many years, Roberta Bitgood, who had written "The Greatest of These Is Love" for his wedding. They had worked together before, I believe. The Session was open to the suggestion that Roberta take over the music ministry at Calvary. She accepted and came to Riverside with her husband, Bert Wiersma, and her daughter, Grace Claire.

When Roberta came, she interviewed each choir member alone and listened to each voice intently. She enjoyed this more intimate way to get to know the choir that would sing for her during two services each Sunday. Choir members could choose which service they wished to sing at or they could sing at both. A quartet of reliable singers—not necessarily soloists—sang the responses. One quartet in the early years was composed of Carol White, soprano; Janet Lynes, alto; Wm. Purcell Gall, tenor; and Cliff Hurley, baritone.

During the time Roberta was at Calvary, the big sanctuary was built and she had the opportunity to plan the specifications for, as well as play on, a new Moller organ, a gift of the Bonnett family. We then had to learn to sing from a divided choir loft, and some had to watch Roberta in a set of mirrors. "Except the Lord Build the House" was written by Roberta for the dedication of the sanctuary. Nell Bell, a choir member, assisted with the choice of words from the scriptures. Her daughter, Carol White, and grandson, Mike White, all sang in the choir, and Mike's daughter has gone on to be a very talented bell ringer who has her own bell choirs.

Of course I remember all the great oratorios we did! The shorter ones we did at the morning service: *Rejoice, Beloved Christians*, by Buxtehude and edited by Clarence Dickinson; and *Job*, written by Roberta herself. The soloists were John Gurney, of Metropolitan Opera fame, and John Ulrich, a talented soloist and choir director. We sang *Sleepers Awake*, by J. S. Bach; *Eucharist* (consisting of music from Wagner's *Parsifal*), arranged by Charlotte Garden with text by John Moment D.D.; *The Song of Amos* by Garden; and a piece by Clokey which had short allegorical numbers about the passion of our Lord. I remember this because Dr. Clokey came to hear us sing this number, and we had a reception for him after the performance. Of course, we sang all the standard oratorios like *Messiah*—Christmas and Easter portions; the Faure *Requiem*; Mendelssohn's *Elijah*, and others.

My experience with Roberta only covers the years from 1952 to 1956, when Richard Gall and I married and moved away. That fall of 1956, Richard and I came back to sing in the small chorus in Bach's *St. Matthew Passion*, which was performed in the new sanctuary.

We sang two anthems each Sunday, and seldom were there soloists. I believe that Roberta felt an anthem was more worshipful than a solo piece, which called attention to the individual. Sometimes she dittoed off the names of the anthems we had sung during the year. I kept one such list but I must have given it to another choir director.

Roberta was also active in the Presbyterian Choir Camp. She was a talented, dedicated Christian musician. She attracted those people of like persuasion, but she also could tell a good joke. It has been a great experience to know her over the years. She is an inspiration.

Vera Ulrich

*Vera's husband, John Ulrich, was a church musician for fifty years.
Together they established an organ memorial fund and
a scholarship program for young musicians.*

My husband John first met Roberta at an AGO meeting in San Bernardino. Roberta had heard a good baritone voice and said she wanted to meet that person. John was a soloist at the Christian Science Church in Riverside and was rather new in the area. So that day Roberta knew she could find a good baritone soloist, and that was the start of a wonderful relationship.

John repaired organs and later went on to direct choral and handbell groups. In Roberta's choir, he sang solos in *Job* and *Messiah* and *St. Matthew Passion,* as well as in many other major works.

One time they both were involved in a production of Beethoven's Ninth Symphony. Roberta was playing viola in the pit while John had the solo part. He had found out only three days before that the performance was to be in German. John didn't know German. So Bert, Roberta's husband, taught him his part in four hours one evening. At the conclusion of the concert, Bert said John was the only one he understood.

Another time, I learned that my voice was changing and needed to sing tenor instead of alto. Roberta allowed me to do this, even though the tenors felt like I was trespassing. Roberta always made us feel comfortable and introduced us to so many wonderful works of music. She had a way of attracting talented musicians.

Mary Lou (Hartsough) Franck

Mary Lou Franck is a retired elementary school music teacher who still teaches music in her church school and sings in the church choir, as well as in the Welsh Choir of Southern California.

Roberta came to Calvary Presbyterian Church in Riverside, California, to be the organist and choir director when I was in my late teens and in college. My dad, Rev. Harold Hartsough, was an associate pastor at the church, and my mother, my sister and I all sang in Roberta's adult choir, for the music was interesting and challenging.

In 1946, *Hymns for Primary Worship* had been published by The Westminster Press. Roberta was on the committee that prepared this book, and she wrote thirty-one hymns for it and arranged nine other songs. My mother, Ruth Jones Hartsough, used this book often in her church school teaching. I have her copy and still use it in teaching music to 3-to-5-year-olds at my church, St. Peter's by the Sea Presbyterian Church, in Rancho Palos Verdes, California.

I'm not sure of the exact date, but possibly it was in the early 1950s—some summer when I was home from college—when my sister Beverly and I sang a duet in church using Roberta's lovely anthem "The Greatest of These Is Love." Years later, when Roberta came to visit Bev, we found out that Roberta had made the duet arrangement specifically for us. What a wonderful thing for her to do and very humbling for us to know.

In August of 1954, I remember that my husband-to-be, Robert Franck, and I searched hard for meaningful but nontraditional music for our wedding. We decided on the "Trumpet Voluntary" by Jeremiah Clark for the processional—dear to us as it was often used for the academic procession at formal assemblies at Occidental College. Roberta helped us settle on the hymn "Thine Is the Glory," by George Frederic Handel, for the recessional. We had many laughs about it as its origin was "Hail the Conquering Hero" from *Judas Maccabeus.* We joked about maybe walking back up the aisle with our hands clasped and arms raised high in triumph.

Beverly (Hartsough) Moulton

Beverly Moulton worked in customer service for Pacific Telephone and sang in church choirs in Riverside, Pasadena, and San Mateo, California. She now lives in Twain Harte, California.

In the early 1950s, Roberta was organist and choir director at Calvary Presbyterian Church in Riverside, California. My father, Harold Hartsough, was the associate pastor. I was around 16 or 17 years old, and my sister Mary Lou was three years older. We both sang in the adult choir and the high school choir.

I remember watching in awe as Roberta would play the organ with such strength and panache! I always thought that the bench should be lowered to make it easier for her to touch the pedals, but it never stopped her. Her legs literally flew over those pedals as she scooted from one end of the bench to the other, still playing the manuals as if she had four hands! Amazing! That's how I remember her.

My sister Mary Lou and I had an opportunity to sing a duet in church back then, and Roberta picked a most beautiful piece for us which she had written herself. It was "The Greatest of These Is Love."

Years later, in 1984, Roberta's daughter, Grace, brought her to our house in Foster City, California, for a visit. Since Mary Lou was visiting me at the time, Roberta accompanied us on our piano as we sang for her. What a joy it was to hear her play again! It was only after we had again sung this duet, "The Greatest of These Is Love," that Roberta surprised us both by telling us that she had arranged the piece for soprano and alto because as teenagers we had begged her to write something for us which we could sing together as a duet. We were so shocked and honored that she would do that for us! She was surprised that we hadn't known all along that the arrangement was done specifically for us.

At the time of my wedding in 1964, Roberta no longer lived in California, but she sent the most perfect gift. It was a musical-note door knocker. We've cherished that knocker over the years by moving it from door to door of every house we've lived in. Thank you, Roberta!

Michael M. White

*Michael White was in high school when Roberta started at Calvary
Presbyterian Church. He sang in the choir and was also the
"sound person," recording all of the choir's concerts.*

During the period that Roberta was at Calvary Presbyterian, I not
only recorded all of the special services, but would also travel with
Roberta to any of her Southern California recitals and record them.

I remember the last cantata that the choir sang was Roberta's
Joseph. We sang it from manuscript since it wasn't yet finished. In fact,
she was making changes to the organ part the morning of the performance. We had recorded it at the rehearsal the Thursday before—
that is, all except the bass solo. The soloist had not arrived from
Germany until that Saturday. I had to record him and splice it into
the tape. That tape along with the manuscript was then sent to the
publisher for the publication of the cantata.

My family had somewhat close ties with Roberta while she was in
Riverside. When the new sanctuary at Calvary was dedicated, Roberta wrote the anthem "Except the Lord Build the House," and my
grandmother compiled the text.

In the mid-1950s my mother and grandmother made a trip to
Europe. While in Paris, they went into a small shop on a side street
and came across a manuscript of ancient music. They brought this
home and gave it to Roberta, who took that piece of music and composed "On an Ancient Alleluia."

The years I spent with Roberta had a great influence on my life.
I learned how to balance music in making recordings. I still sing some
of her solo pieces at Magnolia Presbyterian Church.

Alice Wymer

Alice Wymer still sings solos at age 75 and is director of Children's Choir at First United Methodist Church in Riverside, where she also serves as president of Builders Fellowship and on the Worship, Faith and Fellowship, and Christian Education committees.

There are many memories I have of Roberta and my experiences with her. The first involves her visit to me in my home to invite me to become a member of the choir at Calvary. She brought her dog "Duke" with her. He was a big animal! The first thing he did was to raise his hind leg against one of the stuffed chairs and "do his thing." Roberta was so embarrassed. That got us off to a good start and I was "in." Not only did I have Roberta as a friend, but she was so supportive of my musical endeavors.

As well as singing in the choir, Roberta gave me many opportunities to sing solos in the many oratorios she led us in. I can't begin to name them, but I do remember the work we did to prepare them. Brownie Preston was a tenor in the choir at that time, and he did lots of solo work as well. He has since passed away, but what a glorious voice he had, and such a commitment. (His son, Jerry, drove the school bus on many of the youth trips—to places as far away as Pacific Palisades conference grounds.)

Roberta also provided scholarships for several of us women in the choir to have lessons with Leola Hurlbut in Redlands. Leola was a fine teacher and had a way to help women really develop their voices. Ellen Carter and Phyllis Leighton and I were the lucky ones to receive these scholarships. I am so grateful for that, because I am sure my voice developed beyond my wildest dreams because of that opportunity.

Roberta was a committed Christian and musician. She was always available to provide music herself or see that someone could be counted on to do something special for every kind of meeting held at Calvary.

Her daughter, Grace, young at the time, learned to play flute and was a shining light in all that we did at Calvary. Bert Wiersma, the faithful and wonderful husband and father, was always in the background, but always there.

One of the amusing events for me, was the story she told of a children's choir rehearsal where the children were singing "All Glory, Laud and Honor" in rehearsal and my son, Dale, deigned to add a cha-cha-cha at the end of the first phrase: "All glory, laud and honor to Thee Redeemer King (cha-cha-cha)." Oh well, he at least knew his rhythms.

My husband and I were in Detroit (on our way to a conference in Canada) when Bert had his first heart attack. Roberta knew only one thing to do—that was to carry on with her commitment at her church knowing that Bert was in good hands in the hospital. She loved Bert dearly and knew that she could do nothing but pray, and she did that, and then went on to do what she needed to do. Bert was so proud.

I miss Roberta and know that there are many of us across the world that keep her in our prayers and thoughts.

Shelley Ritchie

Shelley and her husband Andrew Ritchie have taught as lay missionaries in Japan for fourteen years, China for three years, and Kentucky for two years following his retirement from the Air Force in 1979. She is now completing her master's degree in Christian studies at Regent College in Vancouver, British Columbia.

Andrew and I sang under Roberta from 1959 until she left Riverside's Calvary Presbyterian Church around 1961. It was a short time, but it remains the most significant sustained choir experience of my now sixty-four years.

We did Bach's B Minor Mass and premiered her cantata Joseph. It seemed that we were always rehearsing some large work for special presentation. The choir also premiered Dale Wood's anthem "Christ Is Made the Sure Foundation" on the same Sunday that he did it with his own choir at Eden Lutheran Church around the corner. One year, our choir participated in a large choir festival at Redlands University, but I don't recall what we sang. I just remember the moments I sat in silence, in awe at the sound of three hundred voices singing under her direction.

I also enjoyed the time I spent with Roberta working with the music folders. Even though I was not yet a mother, I sang in a local group directed by Roberta called Mother Singers, and I remember doing Pergolesi's *Stabat Mater* with that group.

In the summer of 1960 Roberta enlisted my help as a counselor for a week-long children's choir camp she was directing.

We have exchanged Christmas cards every year since Roberta left Riverside, but have only had the chance to see each other twice in the intervening years. In the mid-1960s we saw Roberta in Midland, Michigan, when Andrew was a graduate student at Michigan State University. Then in the mid-1970s, when we were stationed in Plattsburgh, New York, I had a chance to see Roberta at Lake George, where she was participating in a choir camp.

Robert Derick

A retired church musician, Bob Derick teaches adult education in Riverside, California, and does volunteer work in retirement homes, where he plays the piano, sings songs, and tells "clean stories." He played in the orchestra of the Riverside Opera Company with Roberta and has been associated with her in many other capacities as well. (See Chapter 18 for his reminiscences of Roberta during the thirties.)

Roberta and I—as well as our families—had been close friends in Bloomfield, and we stayed in touch after our move to Riverside and theirs to Buffalo. Then one day I heard that the Calvary Presbyterian Church in Riverside had hired a well-known *woman* organist. No one could remember her name. I knew it couldn't be Roberta, but my curiosity got the best of me and I cornered the pastor and asked. Well, of course, it was the Wiersma tribe!

We renewed our friendship again, and Roberta invited my wife to sing in several affairs. One year, I helped out with a special service involving several choirs.

There were three new pipe organs built in Riverside while Roberta was here, and I do believe she was pushing all the time. Her instrument was a Moller three-manual. Mine was a three-manual Austin. The Methodists came up with a Skinner, also three-manual.

Roberta played viola in the Riverside Symphony and the Riverside Opera orchestra, as well as in AGO programs. I remember conducting one concert when she played violin in the first part and viola in the second. She helped many times with big high school programs and could be counted on to jump in whenever needed.

We did programs together. She accompanied the massed choir and high school chorus in a rather exciting performance of *Rejoice in the Lamb* by Britten.

Grace turned into a knock-out. Flute was her thing but not in the band or orchestra. I had Grace play for me a few times in the big Christmas programs. I knew she would bring an extra touch to whatever I was doing at the time.

Then they left Riverside! A real loss! Things slowed down a bit—I'm no organizer like Roberta but all of us had been active in the AGO, the Riverside Symphony and Opera, and musical events at the University of Redlands.

At length, Roberta came back to Riverside for an AGO event and played a concert on the new organ in the church where I was music director. Grace was with her. Some time later, she returned to Calvary Presbyterian to do a concert that was very well attended.

A few years ago I went to New York City to see my son Peter's debut as a singer with the Metropolitan Opera. I had written to Roberta about it. After the performance, lo and behold, there were Grace and Roberta! They joined us for breakfast the next morning and we spent a lovely time reminiscing.

∽

ᔄ **21** ᔏ

MICHIGAN

Judy Culler

*Judy Culler taught orchestra, general music, and mathematics in the South Red-
ford, Highland Park, Troy, and Livonia school districts, as well as violin, viola,
cello, string bass, and piano privately. She is a deacon and member of the handbell and adult choirs at St. Paul's Presbyterian Church in Livonia, Michigan.*

I met Roberta in September 1960 when I was a first-year teacher
in the South Redford School District near Detroit, Michigan. I was
looking for a church home and read in the newspaper that Roberta
Bitgood was going to be starting as music director and organist at the
Redford Presbyterian Church that next Sunday. I attended the
church service and afterward went down to the choir room to meet
Roberta. I told her that I was a new music teacher in the area and
would like to sing in her choir and that I was a violinist and would
like to play for church services. I was greeted warmly by Roberta, but
I was also handed a hymn book and directed by her to "sing for me."
I sang the alto part in a few hymns while she played, and I guess I
passed the test, as she invited me to attend the next Thursday's choir
rehearsal. Little did I know at the time that this would begin a very
special lifelong friendship for me!

I sang in the choir every Sunday while Roberta lived in Redford,
and I played the violin often with the choir and as a soloist for church
services. I soon learned that Roberta also played the violin and viola,
and we both joined the Detroit Women's Symphony that met in a

church in downtown Detroit on Monday evenings. We played viola together on the second stand of the viola section from 1960 to 1963. We shared in preparing music for many fine concerts during this time. I remember Roberta being particularly impressed when two young men who were the sons of one of the French horn players in the orchestra gave an outstanding performance of the Mozart *Sinfonia Concertante* for violin and viola at one of our concerts.

After dating my husband-to-be, Dave Culler, from June 1961 until June 1962, we were married in Sylvania, Ohio, which was my hometown and the place where Dave was teaching elementary school. Roberta came to Sylvania to play for our wedding, and this pleased both of us very much. We settled in an apartment in Michigan after we were married, and Dave began teaching fifth grade in the Garden City Public Schools, where he stayed for the next thirty years. Roberta always used to say that I knew the choir needed tenors, so I married one!

When Roberta accepted a new calling at the First Presbyterian Church in Bay City, we kept in very close contact with her, often stopping in Bay City on our way to our summer jobs at Interlochen, to sing and play in her church there. Roberta and Bert visited us often at our home in Westland, and Roberta came to Detroit each month for AGO meetings or other events. After most of these meetings, Roberta would spend the night with us and return to Bay City the following day. She had a key to our house, as she often arrived late and we had sometimes gone to bed. I remember one particular time when she came that we didn't realize she was there until morning. When Dave went into the spare bedroom to get his clothes to get dressed for school, there was Roberta asleep in the bed! She woke up as he was looking in the closet and thought she should say something, so she meekly said, "Hello." She says that Dave jumped a few feet off the floor when he heard her!

Many of the nights when Roberta came, we were still awake, however, and we had long visits as I graded math papers and Roberta worked on her ever-present needlepoint. Having a late night snack was always a treat, especially when we had fried chicken, which

Roberta loved. Dave would finally go to bed, and Roberta and I would often stay up a couple more hours. Our first child, Kevin, was born in October 1964, and he grew to love Roberta as we did.

When Roberta was called to her third Michigan church in 1969, the First Congregational Church in Battle Creek, we attended her organ concerts and again sang in her choir whenever we visited. Roberta kept up her viola playing all through the years, and one of her very special highlights was traveling to Europe with the Battle Creek Symphony Orchestra. I remember her saying that she never thought it would be her viola playing that would give her the chance to go to Europe. She loved every minute of this experience. In 1970, our second son, Kurt, was born so we had another Bitgood fan added to our family.

Roberta continued to stay with us when she came to the Detroit area, and there were many nights when she and I would play violin and viola duets just for fun until two in the morning. We were both "night owls," but I can say that Roberta had me beat in this regard. I would give up before she did, and I was thirty years younger!

After Roberta and Bert moved back to Connecticut, we saw them just about every year. During our family vacation in 1977, the four of us stayed for several days in the cabin down by the cove. Whenever we were there on a Thursday night, we went to choir practice, and we always sang in Roberta's choir on Sunday. In addition, I usually played one or two violin solos during the church service. In 1984, when Bert died I was able to be there that week, and I played for his memorial service. Roberta played the organ for the entire service. How many people do we know who could have done that?

In September 1989, Roberta agreed to play for our son Kevin's wedding, here in Livonia. This meant a flight from Connecticut to Michigan for Roberta, a three-day stay here with us, and then a return flight to Connecticut immediately after the wedding so that she could play the organ in church the next day at Crossroads Presbyterian. What dedication! She didn't even get to go to the wedding reception!

In more recent years, I have flown to either Hartford or Providence and rented a car so I could spend a few days with Roberta. Our visiting never seems to end, and our late night duet playing only stopped a couple of years ago. I have been privileged to see all the sights of the New London area and most of Connecticut, and I was included in a wonderful four-day vacation at Tanglewood with Roberta, Grace, and Stuart in 1997.

Roberta will always be one of our very closest friends, and we are proud to be among her hundreds of admirers. She is one exceptional lady!

Jean Frieling

*Jean and her husband, Bob Frieling, were members
of the choir of Redford Presbyterian Church.*

One Sunday service the choir proceeded down the center aisle two by two, singing our first hymn. Our processional came down the aisle, mounted the steps into the sanctuary, and then split off into two sections. At the very end of the processional came one very small boy, three or four years old, who walked at the same pace down the aisle and mounted the steps. Roberta, without missing a beat, beckoned him over and sat him alongside of her on the organ bench, where he stayed for a good part of the service. I wish I could say that our son Peter became an organist, but it is not so. He grew up to be an engineer like his father, and he has a beautiful wife and two nearly grownup ones of his own.

We moved to the little town of Farmington, and became busy rearing children and raising Springer Spaniel puppies. Bert and Roberta visited us often and became like family. One of my Springers was returned to me. She was a pretty little female and I didn't know what to do with her, because I already had two adult dogs. When Bert and Roberta said they would take her, we were delighted. Some time later, after they had gone to Connecticut, Roberta wrote that she and Suzie went for their daily swim in the cove. Lucky dog.

Rev. Janet A. Lee

*Janet Lee has been Minister of Music and the Arts at Hillsdale First United
Methodist Church for the last twelve years. As Diaconal Minister, she served
at Clawson United Methodist Church for twenty-five years and is a past-
president of the National Fellowship of United Methodists in Worship,
Music and Other Arts.*

I have two memories of the times when Roberta lived in the Detroit area. I met her for the first time at a Michigan Federated Music
Clubs state board meeting. We were seated next to each other for
lunch. I was a very young mother serving as state choral chairman and
couldn't imagine myself eating with and talking with such an outstanding person as Roberta Bitgood. But by the end of the meal I realized that the reason she was so highly revered by her colleagues was
because no one was a stranger to her. I felt as if I had always known
her. And from that moment on I knew I had gained a new friend.

Roberta was an encourager and I was a recipient of that encouragement time and again after that initial meeting. I like to compose,
and though I was not very good at it, Roberta kept encouraging me
along the way. I appreciated her generosity and felt a great loss when
she moved back east. Even then she kept in touch and was always
ready and willing to share conversations by telephone or by mail.

Thank you, Roberta!

Alan Crabtree

*During a thirty-five year transportation career, including positions with the
Canadian National Railways and Canadian Transportation Commission,
Alan Crabtree served churches in Cayuga, Toronto, Sudbury, North Bay,
Windsor, Detroit, Paris, and Ottawa. He is retired and is currently
the organist and director of music at the Annesley United Church.*

I first met Roberta in 1960 at the AGO national convention in
Detroit. Later, upon moving to Windsor, I decided to join the Detroit
AGO chapter. As soon as she saw me, Roberta remarked, "Here's my
Canadian friend."

Then, when I was living in Ottawa, I suggested to the local chapter of the Royal Canadian College of Organists that they bring in Roberta to do a workshop and a clergy-organist type of event. Roberta agreed, and her accommodations were a suite at the fancy Chateau-Laurier. Knowing that she was fond of ice cream sundaes, I had a huge mountain of ice cream decked out with hot fudge, butterscotch, marshmallow, and whipped cream delivered to her by room service during one of her breaks. The committee all showed up with miniature versions of the same thing to keep her company while she launched into her gigantic dessert, which she was more than able to finish!

I remember calling Roberta to arrange a visit with her in 1996. She said, "Too bad you can't come this Sunday. I'm having cataract surgery on Friday and haven't found a substitute." As far as I know, she did play that service herself, from memory.

Jean Nykamp

Jean Nykamp is a retired school music teacher who was filling in as choir director of First Presbyterian Church in Bay City when Roberta was hired. She lives in the same home in Essexville that she has occupied for thirty-six years.

When Roberta came to First Presbyterian, my own children were five, seven, and nine, and I had been directing the children's choirs from the balcony since there was no room for them on the main floor. Because of this, Roberta had a ready and willing assistant from the time she arrived.

I remember that the children wore little white surplices with just their street clothes down below, and Roberta thought they looked like nightgowns. It wasn't long before she had me measuring each child in grades one through three for new red robes!

One thing I appreciated was that Roberta emphasized the singing of hymns with the young people, which was something they hadn't done much before. Every Sunday that the children sang, Roberta would type up the whole service for them, including all the words of the responses, the Doxology, and everything else. It was a lot of extra work, but it paid off.

I also observed that the children were never allowed to sing in a loud raucous tone or to force their voices, and the result was such a pure, beautiful sound. The children did a cantata on two occasions each year—Christmas Eve and Palm Sunday afternoon. And each spring there was a junior choir festival. Roberta helped organize the Bay Area Choristers' Guild chapter, and was on the National Board of Choristers' Guild at that time.

Thanks to Roberta, I was able to attend Choristers' Guild workshops, and for this I am eternally grateful, since it was this form of continuing education that helped me get back into teaching after some time off.

When Roberta first took the reins, some of the men in the adult choir were in the habit of taking a smoking break in the middle of choir rehearsal. Roberta put a stop to this and lost a few men over it, but she gained a few too and used some of the "low women" to sing tenor.

Roberta kept close track of attendance. Nelda Taylor was the librarian for the adult choir and also took attendance. Somehow Nelda always managed to have the best attendance—100%—and people joked that it was because she kept the records.

The choir performed major works and the rehearsals for them went on pretty late—once until nearly 11 p.m. Roberta was very fussy about the processional and did not allow the choir to "waddle like ducks." So they rehearsed walking elbow to elbow.

The choir year ended with a choir banquet. At the last one before the Wiersmas moved to Battle Creek, Roberta came out dressed in a long gown, with a floppy handkerchief in her hand and a feather in her hair, and sang a hilarious rendition of "Lo, Hear the Gentle Lark" complete with all the trills. It brought down the house.

One of the last things Roberta did before she left was to oversee the purchase of handbells. They were used in several performances by various age groups, including Roberta's last Christmas there.

I remember the "dear little house" not far from the church which

Roberta and Bert bought. They had painted and fixed it up real cute. Bert had a heart attack right about the time they moved and by then everything had been moved out of the house. Bert was in the hospital and Roberta was commuting back and forth from Battle Creek. I don't know how she did it.

Roberta and the minister, Rev. Hugh Schuster, got along very well, but the big drawback of the job was the old clunker of an organ. When it was finally replaced years later, Roberta came back to do the dedicatory recital.

I don't think I ever cried harder than I did when Roberta and Bert left Bay City. I didn't know how I'd be able to manage without Roberta, and after all these years I still consider her a very dear and cherished friend.

Carl Mezoff

Born and raised in Bay City, Carl Mezoff runs a small architecture and engineering practice in Stamford, Connecticut. While he has not kept up his organ playing, he has sustained an avocation in music by singing with the Pro Arte Singers, the only professional chorus in Connecticut, whose recordings are available on cassette and compact disc.

My memories of Roberta go back to a period when I was in high school, in the early sixties. Dr. Bitgood had just come to Bay City, Michigan, to take up the post of organist of the First Presbyterian Church, the most prominent church in town. As I recollect, the Presbyterian church had a large, old, and rather clunky four-manual organ that had been assembled out of bits and pieces of several abandoned organs. I had been taking lessons from the organist at the Lutheran church for several years when "Dr. B" arrived. Being a rather raw teenager I had utterly no knowledge of her illustrious history, and assumed, in a matter of fact way, that I was merely getting a new teacher.

At our first meeting the thing that impressed me most was her incredible Boston accent, which was a wonder to my young Midwestern ears. Something about how she formed her *R*'s with her upper lip was endlessly fascinating to me. I took weekly lessons from Dr. B for about two years, between 1963 and 1965, but I am afraid that I was a rather indifferent pupil, having more interest at the time in basketball and baseball than in Bach.

In spite of my lack of diligence, by sheer force of will Dr. B was eventually able to prepare me for a performance competition, the prize for which was a scholarship to the National Music Camp at Interlochen, Michigan. I remember the horrendous stage fright of the competition event. The audition was held in a small chapel on an electronic organ. Even now I can recall the feel of the slippery keys under my clammy fingers. My intense fear caused me to begin at a speed I had never attempted before. I sprinted through the piece, one of Bach's eight little preludes and fugues—the D minor—at a harrowing pace, with my heart pounding in my ears. Somehow I got through it on autopilot without flubbing. One of the judges commented that my "changes in registration" were not very smooth. I recall with delight Roberta snickering at that, because there had not been any changes in registration! In any case, I was lucky enough to win a scholarship to camp that summer, thanks to her.

At some point in this period, Roberta played a major concert at the Presbyterian church for which I was selected to turn pages. The entire town was invited. As the date for the concert approached, it began to dawn on me that this was something I definitely did not want to do. I became certain I would die before the concert was over. I knew that with one false move on my part the concert would come to a screeching halt, and the whole world would know why. The organ console in that church is normally completely concealed behind an enormous bench on which the minister sits when not at the pulpit. I eventually got up the courage to agree to the job, knowing that at least I would be safely hidden from the eyes of the audience behind this barrier.

When I followed Dr. B out into the enormous sanctuary filled with thousands of applauding audience members, I was horrified to see that the minister's bench and pulpit had been removed so that the organ was now totally exposed. My stomach jumped into my throat and my legs turned to jelly, for I knew that certain death now awaited. I recall my shaking hand turning the pages of the first several pieces, luckily without incident, and feeling my heart rate decline to about 250 beats per minute. Then, I saw that the music for the next piece was decorated with paperclips, and tried vainly to recall what I had been told about repeats and cuts. After two pages I saw Dr. B nod for the first paperclip. I couldn't remember whether I was to go back for a repeat or forward for a cut and I guessed wrong! I frantically turned back realizing I should have gone forward, all the while Dr. B's fingers and feet continued to fly over the keys from memory. Somewhere in my dim consciousness I could hear her calling out and signaling with her head to turn the other way. My arm got caught in the folds of the overly large choir robe that I had been given, and the sweat on my face was causing my glasses to slide down my nose. Eventually, when Dr. B had a hand free, she calmly reached up and turned to the correct spot, never missing a note. I have no memory how we got through the remainder of the concert, but I will be eternally grateful for her having saved me from disgrace.

My organ studies with Dr. B were cut short by my father's job transfer to Europe. Several years later, Dr. B paid our family a visit in Kusnacht, Switzerland—this was probably during the summer of '67 or '68. She stayed with us for several days, giving us a chance to tour historic churches and play several of the organs in downtown Zurich.

William D. Kaltrider

Bill Kaltrider is the organist and choir director at St. Mary's Catholic Church in Alpena, Michigan. He also plays funerals at St. John the Baptist Catholic Church, as well as playing, on occasion, at the cathedral in Gaylord.

Although our paths crossed many times over the past fifty-plus years, I distinctly remember my first meeting with Roberta. It was at the Waldenwoods School of Sacred Music, and I learned the Bach G minor Prelude and Fugue under her guidance. This was in the early

1940s! Swimming and roller-skating were the extent of the physical activities at Waldenwoods. I couldn't swim and Roberta couldn't skate, so I learned to swim from Roberta and she roller-skated—hanging on to me for dear life.

My next contact with Roberta was when she was in Riverside. I was fresh out of the U.S. Navy, not knowing what I wanted to do with my life. I worked for the Alfred Kilgen Organ Company in Los Angeles and played in a little Baptist church in Eagle Rock. I took a lesson from Roberta as often as I could get something prepared. I learned the Farnam "Toccata" and the Bach Fugue a la Gigue at that time. My church had a Wurlitzer reed-electronic. The action was sooo slow. Roberta still had the little Roosevelt in Riverside. She brought all my complaining to a halt when she said, "I'll never let an organ keep me from playing any music I want to play!"

I remember most fondly my times with Roberta and Bert when they were in Bay City, Michigan. I owned and operated a music store located some fifty miles from Bay City. The two of them would often go canoeing on a Sunday afternoon and appear at our door—sometimes at suppertime. It was on one of these occasions that I learned to make Bitgood Burgers. Take one pound of hamburger, lots of chopped onion, and add a lot of water (almost soup); spread this on hamburger buns; place under the broiler. You can easily feed 5,000!

It was through these informal times that I got to know Bert. He loved his work as an occupational therapist, but one day was telling me of a problem he was unable to solve for one of his patients. This young high school boy was an excellent trumpet player. He had been playing with firecrackers and blew the fingers off of both hands. Bert was determined to find a way for him to play the trumpet again. I worked with Bert in designing solenoid magnets and a special switch he could operate with his thumb—and then talked a local electric motor company into producing it. This was really exciting for all concerned. It also cemented our friendship.

It was during this time that I was Roberta's assistant at First Presbyterian. This was my first experience working with a Bitgood Summer Choir. The format was that Roberta would pick out two easier anthems, and the title and composer would appear in the Sunday printed bulletin. With no weekday rehearsal we would meet whoever showed up that Sunday morning at 10 a.m., rehearse them into a choir, and then at 11 a.m., "You're on."

Because of Roberta's responsibilities with the AGO, she would call on me to fill in at various times of the year. One of these times was late in January. Because of the time of year and the distance involved to my home, I would often stay at their house. This particular January, I walked in and there to greet me was their Christmas tree! Well, having nothing else to do on Saturday night, and not wanting to let an opportunity slip by, I went into town, bought lots of pink paper, and when they came home the next week they were greeted by the biggest Valentine Tree ever created. I understand they brought many choir people in to see what happens if you leave your Christmas tree up too long.

Melvin Rookus

Melvin Rookus is the organist and director of music at the Nardin Park United Methodist Church in Farmington Hills, Michigan. He directs a program that has ten choirs, a music staff of four, and a music series comprising sixteen annual concerts.

I first met Dr. Bitgood in 1963 while an organ student at the University of Michigan. I'd heard of the bi-annual organ auditions held by the Detroit Council of Churches through which church search committees and organists looking for positions could come together in a setting that benefited each party. The location was the large First Baptist Church on Woodward Avenue. Scared to death of the big city, the big church, and the big organ, I took my turn at the console. While I can't remember what my prepared pieces were, I vividly recall Roberta stepping forward with a handwritten hymn-tune (melody only) and asking me to play it with harmonization, and then inviting an improvisation on the tune. When I was finished, she offered a quick comment: "Not too bad, young man—in fact, rather good." I was thrilled. As a result, I obtained the position of organist at the First Presbyterian Church in Farmington, a placement that was to determine the following events in my life in so many ways.

When Roberta took the position at the First Presbyterian Church in my hometown, Bay City, Michigan, I made it a point to contact her right after she moved. We quickly established a strong relationship, enjoying the inevitable Scrabble games into the wee hours of the morning, as well as gossiping about people in the music circles. Roberta was following my first organ teacher H. R. "Rusty" Evans, who had held that post since 1929, and had a rather loyal following. The four-manual instrument was simply an instrument that defied description, having been a personal project of Mr. Evans. Roberta endured times of extreme stress dealing with every type of problem known to an organist or an organ technician. Later, it was with great pride that Roberta returned to First Presbyterian to dedicate the new Casavant, long after she had left Bay City. However, people there still remember her gray car with the canoe on top, for Roberta and Bert loved to depart right after the postlude to head for the nearby and numerous waterways to explore their favorite outdoor endeavors. As always, she became involved in numerous musical activities, including the trip to Saginaw to play in the local symphony orchestra.

Roberta played for my wedding in 1967 at the First Presbyterian Church in Farmington, Michigan. At the rehearsal dinner, she remarked on the challenges she faced in preparing prelude music that included the Mendelssohn Third Sonata and other "favorites" of the groom—all on a rather restricted two-manual Allen organ. We later shared many laughs over those wedding decisions!

In 1966, being young and adventurous (along with having a few dollars from my first year of public school teaching), I traveled to Europe for eight weeks. Through dialogue with Roberta and Bert, I discovered they were making plans for their first trip to Great Britain. Our schedules overlapped by a few days. Picking up a pre-ordered Austin Healey 3000 sports car—a convertible—I met them at their London hotel. Roberta immediately ordered the top down, placed

Bert in the passenger seat, and climbed into the rear jump seat. Around London we went, with Roberta pointing, shouting, and enjoying the sight of the London landmarks. I was really too nervous about driving to be embarrassed by the spectacle we must have made, especially when a Bobby redirected our escapade through Hyde Park.

I recall spending an evening in Battle Creek, Michigan, when the conversation with Bert, and my wife, Ann, turned toward AGO leadership—in short, high office positions—and specifically the presidency. Ann, a non-musician, turned to Roberta and said that certainly she would attain that position. Roberta was adamant that lofty positions were held only by the male species (or something akin). Thus, we were delighted when Roberta wrote to inform us of her newly elected position as president of the American Guild of Organists. She reminded Ann of her earlier skepticism, but thanked her for her faith in the matter. Both of us were thrilled.

I'm sure close confidants and friends know of Roberta's frugal ways. We helped her pack for her final move back to Quaker Hill. I truly can't describe how many boxes we packed that contained 90% empty jars of instant coffee, partially filled Kleenex containers, and other similar items. Roberta would simply not be wasteful! If that sounds unbelievable, one only had to eat with her. A chicken would be reduced to a small pile of bones. And of course the ultimate was to share a fresh lobster dinner at her favorite hangout in Noank, Connecticut. For a Midwestern rookie, I was quickly taught that there was more to lobster than just the tail. The first time we did this turned out to be the lengthiest and messiest dinner I have ever eaten. But truly delightful!

It would be difficult to know Roberta without asking her to write a composition. I myself have been honored to commission two works. The first was in honor of a retiring pastor at the Grace Lutheran Church in Pontiac, Michigan, where I was director of music. "Lord, May We Follow" has been widely used and I always have felt pride in having a degree of ownership in that work. The second piece was written for the choirs of the Nardin Park United Methodist Church in Farmington Hills, Michigan, where I hold my current position. "Great Is God" was a milestone for Roberta because, in her words, it was her first $1.00 anthem. When she came to Farmington Hills to direct the first "performance," she charmed both kids and adults with her humor and insightful remarks. The weekend festivities also included a church dinner at which Roberta and I put together a program of music for two pianos. Of course, she selected the music and we must have played for close to an hour—more than many in attendance had bargained for—but then, as Roberta put it, "They got their money's worth."

On one of our visits to her Quaker Hill home, we carefully made our way down the hill to the old cabin, for many years her summer retreat. Several games of Scrabble lasted until midnight, when Roberta invited me to take in the Long Island Sound via canoe. Since I grew up with a cabin in Northern Michigan which was located on a rather fast river, I was intrigued to try open waters. With Roberta in the rear, off we went. The sights and sounds of the Coast Guard Academy were simply awesome. The lights of New London were magnificent on this July evening. But after close to two hours, my arms were sore, my back ached, and Roberta was ready to proceed even further. It took more than a few pleas to garnish the return trip, where Ann and Bert were just a tad concerned—in fact, ready to call for emergency help. Roberta was quite indignant that they would question our stability, mental as well as physical.

I always kept Roberta on the church mailing list so as to keep her apprised of our musical offerings and activities. It was always so nice to hear from her in that unique scrawling handwriting or on the manual typewriter which would fill every inch of paper. She was always one to compliment and encourage. Her Christmas letter, too, is always a classic, and perhaps the only one I get that takes several readings to digest. What a great person!

Nelda Taylor

Nelda Taylor taught English for 43 years. She was invited to join the First Presbyterian choir by its director, Rusty Evans, who taught in the same high school. She sang in the First Presbyterian choir for 50 years and was the choir librarian for 30 of them.

I remember a sign that said "COUNT!" that was fastened to the back of the organ when Roberta was choir director of First Presbyterian. Also, I so much admired Roberta's ability to pull a program together, even when it seemed impossible.

One Christmas Eve, the electricity went out during the 11 p.m. service while Roberta was at the organ. Undeterred, she continued on by candlelight, directing an a capella version of "Wise Men, Seeking Jesus," due of course to the organ's being without power.

Margaret Unger

Margaret Unger is enjoying an active retirement after earning graduate degrees in both music and library science and teaching strings, fourth grade, and elementary vocal music for twenty-six years, as well as working as a librarian. She still plays the viola in the Cadillac Orchestra, Benzie Symphonette, and other "odd jobs."

When Roberta and I played in the Saginaw Symphony, I used to ride with her to rehearsals and we would always enjoy a "salad stop" at an Italian restaurant on the way home.

I remember that Roberta's Christmas tree always stayed up a long time, and it would frequently end up with valentines on it.

After the Wiersmas moved to Battle Creek, I would stop there with my family on our way to Illinois for Christmas and we would have lunch with Roberta and Bert at the Howard Johnsons off the freeway. Roberta always made me feel it was nothing for her to rearrange her schedule in order to fit in these get-togethers.

When Roberta came back to Bay City to play the new Casavant organ at First Presbyterian in 1984, we were very pleased to have her stay with us.

Arliss Benham

Arliss Benham, a retired consumer consultant, is the organist of St. Paul
Lutheran Church in Battle Creek. She teaches a Bible class and is a public
speaker and retreat leader, a volunteer pianist and organist
in nursing homes, and a published writer.

My first meeting with Roberta Bitgood was at the First Congregational Church in Battle Creek. A mutual friend of ours, David Sly, had arranged for her to give me organ lessons. Because of a devastating personal experience, my self-esteem at the time was at minus 100, and when I walked into that massive church and sat down at the huge three-manual pipe organ, my heart was beating so rapidly that I didn't even need a metronome. Then Roberta sat down and played several hymns for me. It was awesome, breathtaking—and I felt an exciting challenge to learn.

Dr. Bitgood, your inspiration has lived with me for more than these twenty years. Your encouragement has given me courage until now, when one of my greatest dreams has come true—at last I have the privilege of sitting at one of those three-manual instruments, and I lose myself over and over again. Thank you!

One episode that sticks in my mind occurred during one of my lessons. Roberta used to stand at the back of the church and listen as I played. Those who know about Bach's organ music know that it keeps both hands, both feet, and the mind in a whirl. It is very scriptural, for "the right hand knoweth not what the left hand doeth"— that is, the left hand playeth independently from the right foot, while the left foot countermelodies with the right hand. Dr. Bitgood, master of the pipe organ that she was, called out from the back of the sanctuary, "Wait a minute, Arliss, you missed a rest two measures back in the right hand."

Now, in the workshops I teach, I use this example in reference to the Bible passage where Jesus said to His disciples, "Come apart with me by yourself to a quiet place and rest a little while." *Sometimes, in life as in music, the rests are more important than the notes.* What a master-teacher she was! What a friend! What an inspiration!

Beryl Garn

Beryl Garn, a longtime associate organist at First Congregational Church in Battle Creek, is still teaching piano students at age 96.

Roberta has been a dear friend for many, many years and is a person for whom I have had a great admiration as a musician and caring person.

When she and Bert attended their first AGO meeting in Southwestern Michigan, we were in for a surprise! They said, "Hi" and then disappeared. It was a dinner potluck meeting and when it came time to eat, we waited and worried and wondered what had happened to them. Finally they reappeared and said that they had taken a boat ride and couldn't find the dock in the dark! From then on we knew that if our meeting was anywhere near water, that canoe would arrive with them, riding on top of their car.

We attended many concerts, masterclasses, and conventions together. One recital was the dedication of the new organ at Hope College in Holland, Michigan. It was winter and there was a lot of snow. We enjoyed the recital but as we left town, Roberta said she didn't think she had enough gas in the car to get home. It was late and everyone had left, so we drove around town looking for an open station—no luck! However, Roberta did notice one service station with a house attached to it. After many calls and knocks on the door, the owner came out and saved us!

Nothing daunted Roberta. Bert told me once about her looking for a gas station late one rainy night in Detroit when she was alone and dressed in a long evening gown, as was the style then. Bert admired her so much.

Roberta had a wonderful sense of humor. At any given time she could find something different or comical. We laughed a great deal.

I was a piano major who took some organ in college as an extra instrument, never thinking I would use or pursue it. However, when an organist was needed for the children's and youth chapel services, I studied with each new organist at First Congregational in Battle

Creek from 1945 on, and kept on with it as associate organist while also substituting in many churches in Battle Creek. Roberta was such a help with suggestions and ideas in interpretation. I will always appreciate it!

Fran Delmerico Isaac

Fran Isaac taught music in public school and is a veteran choir member at First Congregational Church in Battle Creek, where she currently directs two handbell choirs.

It's no wonder that Roberta's Christmas card list is so long—she has so many friends because she herself is a good friend. While admiring her capabilities, we all have greatly enjoyed her penchant for telling stories and her keen sense of humor.

She and Bert were very hospitable, and chancel choir members in Battle Creek enjoyed a frequent informal "open house" in their cozy, comfortable home. After Sunday service Roberta would say, "Bert has a turkey leg (or something similar) in the oven. Wouldn't you like to share it with us?" I would quickly find something to add to Bert's preparations. I remember the good food and conversations during those Sunday dinners!

While carrying out her duties as organist, director of childrens' and adult choral groups, and of handbell choirs, Roberta played with the Battle Creek Symphony and took an active part in the Morning Musical and Altrusa clubs, as well as AGO. At the same time, she was also quietly giving free organ lessons to young people in our church who she thought showed potential. Had more organists done this, we might not be having the current acute shortage of organists in Michigan.

There is one story that always elicits a chuckle from Battle Creek Symphony Orchestra members with whom she traveled to Europe. Most of the time we stayed with families in the cities where we played, but in London, where we did not play, we were mistakenly booked into a sub-standard hotel. One evening Roberta brought a "doggy-bag" of French fries back to the hotel. During the night, those of us who shared the dormitory-style room assigned to us were awakened by a persistent, scratchy sound. Finally Roberta realized that a friendly mouse had discovered her bag of "perfectly good French fries," which she had not wanted to waste!

Gary Tallenger

Gary Tallenger was the tour director of the Battle Creek Symphony Orchestra during its 1974 European tour.

Roberta toured with great enthusiasm as a violist on our symphony tour of Continental Europe and England for twenty-three days in July of 1974. She enjoyed the countries and sights, the home stays, and the camaraderie of a great group of her musical peers.

If her enthusiasm was compromised in any manner, this would have been related to the effort involved in making her legs and feet cooperate. She usually elected less far-reaching jaunts from the bus than others would take, just to be sure she could be back aboard on time. But all that judicious behavior was put aside when we reached the old walled city of York, England. The bus dropped everyone off outside the walls, of course. The walkways were of traditional cobblestone, and there were few flat stretches. Roberta was not to be denied any access and led the charge through the narrow passages. She was determined to see the famous York Minster cathedral, and hear the organ if possible. Back on the bus, on time, she reported to all that she had done that, and seen the entire city within the walls also. She even passed me up at one time! All her buddies were struggling to keep pace. The entire busload applauded her joyful report. I think she had, for a moment, been to Mecca!

Once again, those of us who fondly remember Roberta cheer her endurance!

163

Margaret (Byrens) Kuiper

*Margaret Kuiper is the eldest of the seven children of Danford and Emily
Byrens. She is a married kindergarten teacher with seven children of her own.*

I have a fond memory of Roberta as a violist. I am a cellist and
was in the Battle Creek Symphony with her when I was in high
school. I was always amazed and amused at the way Roberta sat while
playing the viola. She would lean back in her chair with her legs
crossed. The foot crossed over would have the shoe (loafer) off and
she would be swinging it around her foot while she played. She could
be playing a very difficult passage and wouldn't miss a beat, but
meanwhile the shoe would be swinging. It was fun to watch and I've
never seen that style of playing since then.

Barry Evans

*Barry Evans was a choir member in Battle Creek when she got to know
Roberta, and was also one of her organ students for a while. She is now in her
eighties and lives in an assisted living facility. She still sings in her church choir.*

I remember:

Roberta's incredible energy and enthusiasm not only for our
church choir but also the Battle Creek Symphony, all AGO activities, and musical events for miles around.

Her sense of humor, which would lighten up choir rehearsals
with remarks such as "Altos are defined as Low Women Who Sing"
and the inevitable "… or else I'll sing the part myself!"

The fearlessness she displayed when she ran out of gas one night
after an organ recital in Ann Arbor and accepted a ride from a truck-
er to get to a gas station in Jackson.

The special anthem she wrote for the retirement of my husband
David. We both felt greatly honored by this.

Rhenda Pease

Rhenda Pease has been an organist for many years in Kalamazoo, Michigan, where she also has a full-time private music studio. She is ensemble chairman for the Michigan Music Teachers' Association and Southwest Michigan chairman for the National Guild of Piano Teachers.

In the 1970s, when Roberta resided in Battle Creek, she always attended the Southwestern Michigan AGO meetings. I particularly remember a year-end June picnic and officer installation meeting. I still smile when I think of Roberta's being the first member to don her swimsuit that warm June night. She jumped into the backyard pool at our host's home and then proceeded to encourage everyone else to waste no time in joining her for a refreshing splash. I've always been impressed by her uninhibited enjoyment of life!

And I've always been honored to be on her gigantic Christmas mailing list.

Reflections on Roberta Bitgood Wiersma

Roberta is not "just" a bit good,
She's a fantastic phenomenon!
Her "sanguine" persona overflows with fabulous
      friendship for all!
She has a heart of gold—a mind so creative
Always her pen is full of artistic notes—
Creating scores of *scores* of sonorous overtones.
Let me sing a clear "pitch" for this most inspiring
      musician—
She gathers respect and love from us average souls
Who strive to bring beauty to our world.
All the while she readily dispenses a God-given genius
In all areas of life—in her prolific composing,
In her keyboard music-making, her myriad of church
      services,
Likewise, recitals—even at age 91!

In her choral conducting, and in her public speaking which
Sparkles with her fundamentally quick witted humor
Bespeaking her love for life.
As in glorious triadic progression, so Roberta's life of
Creativity is a succession of running sixteenths—full of
      vigor, expressing
A joyous crescendo as her life in accelerando, now begins
      to slow to a
Stately pace—a life always rooted in the Heavenly Source.
Her praiseful melodies recapitulate thankfulness to the
      Lord above for
Life—for Love—for Music Sublime!
I thank God for her special touch on my life!

Friends in Battle Creek

*David Graham served one church in Massachusetts before accepting his call to
First Congregational Church in Battle Creek, where he still serves as Minister of
Parish Care. His wife Pat and their daughters sang under Roberta's direction in
choir programs and other local musical productions. Ben Davis was a boy sopra-
no and played in Roberta's handbell group at First Congregational. His mother,
Jane Davis, was a teacher and sang with her husband in Roberta's adult choir.
Ben still works in Battle Creek, while Jane has retired and lives in Florida. Judy
Taylor became interested in singing again through the achievements of her daugh-
ter, who enjoyed special encouragement as a member of Roberta's youth choir.
Judy is now program director of the Battle Creek Girls' Chorus and still sings in
the First Congregational choir. Helen Brownell, who retired from her work with
emotionally disturbed children, now volunteers in the church office at First
Congregational, and is still singing in the choir after 55 years.*

Rev. David and Pat Graham, who are still at First Congregational
Church in Battle Creek, recount that despite a cluttered desk, Roberta could put her hands on whatever it was she needed.

Pat was often a soloist for Roberta's special musical programs
around town. One time she had to sing after a luncheon and was too
nervous to eat. After Pat finished singing her numbers, Roberta
looked at her and said, "You should have 'et'!"

David and Pat appreciated that when their daughter was having difficulty getting a job after graduate school, Roberta told her to keep trying—that she herself had had about one hundred rejections of her musical compositions for every one that was accepted. This was very worthwhile encouragement.

Ben Davis, who sang in a children's choir under Roberta, relates that during one rehearsal when Roberta was having trouble getting the singers to count, she posed the question, "What does any choir director in the world ask of their choir members?"

After a pause, Ben said, "Take the gum out of your mouth."

At that, Roberta roared with laughter, and agreed, "That, too."

Jane Davis, mother of Ben and Becky, recalls Roberta's recruiting her to cue the boy bellringers in Battle Creek. It was Thanksgiving Eve and they were playing "Jesu, Joy of Man's Desiring" with Roberta at the organ. Jane was to stand by the boys to bring them in at the right time—when Roberta played *"doo, dool, dee, doo, dool, dee."* Jane counted and announced to the boys, "Get ready, set, *now!*" At that, the boys *all* turned around, looked at Jane, and said, *"Now?"* Jane reports that they did get it together for the rest of the piece.

Judy Taylor, from Battle Creek, remembers that Roberta put music in her voice—what a real gift. Roberta would transpose on the spur of the moment if a vocalist was having a problem with range. What a wonderful sense of humor she had, says Judy. She especially remembers Roberta doing a hysterically funny show with hand puppets.

Helen Brownell treasures the memory of several visits to the Wiersmas in Connecticut. During those visits she sometimes went into New York City with Roberta. While Roberta attended AGO meetings, Helen would wander around the streets of the city. One time she walked into St. Patrick's Cathedral. A young lady was playing the organ. She stopped and asked if Helen was visiting New York. Helen answered that she was, and that she was tagging along with Roberta Bitgood. The young woman jumped off the organ bench and said, "I've always wanted to meet that wonderful woman." How proud

Helen says she felt, to think that she was a friend of Roberta's. She feels very fortunate to have sung under Roberta, and believes that "Roberta has forgotten more music than most anyone will ever know."

David Sly

A full time counselor at Olivet Middle School, David Sly is also director of music at First United Methodist Church in Marshall, Michigan. He says he is an organist because Roberta told him he could! He is a tenor soloist as well.

I consider Dr. Roberta Bitgood to be a woman of extreme talent and intellect. She has been a mentor and leader in the church music field forever and will always be in my thoughts and heart as I take the bench and redirect the choir every Sunday.

At my first meeting with Roberta, she had been charged to get some younger members in the Guild. "You must join the AGO. *We need you!*" This was a much warmer greeting in 1971 than that of the Draft Board!

Join the AGO I did. Roberta next decided for me that I should have an office in the local chapter. Roberta and the board needed a treasurer and so I was elected. I was in between graduate school and a teaching position in public school music and was exchanging my services taking care of animals for a room. These animals included many cats.

The AGO records were left at my room in a box, and we all know what purpose cats have for a box! When I called Roberta with the news of the cats' use of our AGO records, she simply gave her wonderful full-teeth-and-body howl and said, "Call Kay Christian, she will know what to do." From that moment on and for many years to follow, Kay Christian was our wonderfully talented AGO treasurer of the Southwest Michigan chapter. Roberta has tremendous faith in the power of people, one of her finest gifts.

Roberta is a wonderful character. The very first time I heard her in recital as an adult was at the First Congregational Church in Battle Creek. She did a program of early American tunes, making her grand entrance to the console in full cowgirl outfit complete with firing cap guns. Roberta did not, however, wear cowgirl boots for the organ pedal work. What a recital!

When I was a kid so many years ago in Midland, I heard about this fabulous woman organist in Bay City at the First Presbyterian Church. My aunt took me to hear Roberta. Little did I know that we would meet again as adults and that she would be so gracious, kind, and such a gifted inspiration to me all my life.

Roberta was program chair one year in the Southwest Michigan AGO chapter. "We need to do a major work with Guild singers and their church choir members," she said. The Durufle *Requiem* was performed with Roberta conducting and Esther Manni playing the organ accompaniment so sensitively and Roberta floating around the chancel of Kalamazoo's First United Methodist Church chanting, "You sound just like angels in Heaven." For another Guild program, she did the children's work "100% Chance of Rain." She had made a strong suggestion that "David Sly needs to accompany this!" and so I did. Roberta again brought out the best in every person with whom she came in contact. She loved AGO dinner meetings and great discussions about church "stuff."

Roberta did a whole program of Bitgood music while in Battle Creek. I was honored to be asked to sing her solo piece "The Greatest of These Is Love." I still cherish the copy she signed for me, "To my favorite tenor, David Sly." I know she had a favorite tenor every place she landed, but she will always remain my favorite church musician. A very special place in my memory and heart are sealed for the one and only Dr. Roberta Bitgood.

Soli Deo Gloria

Helen Hammond

Helen Hammond taught in Kansas and Arizona before moving to Battle Creek. She has four favorite vacation spots since her children and grandchildren live in Idaho, Arkansas, Florida, and Michigan.

When I was state president of the Michigan Federated Music Clubs, I wanted desperately to get an official state song. We had a contest and must have gotten fifty entries. Some had guitar accompaniment, some even had birds! Roberta and several other judges heard them all and narrowed it down to five finalists. I sang them at the district meetings and gave members a chance to vote on the one they thought was most suitable. We decided on "Michigan, the Water Wonderland" by Phil Hadrill, but never succeeded in getting it through the committee. Michigan still doesn't have a state song. I even entered one. We should have had Roberta compose one!

Roberta was my state choral director for the massed chorus while I was president. I remember that during a state convention at the Michigan Education Association Center near St. Mary's Lake, she directed "Gifts from the Sea," written by one of her students, Julia Crawford Goodfellow.

Roberta directed the Morning Musical Chorus also, and we practiced in her choir room at First Congregational Church. With her perfect pitch, she couldn't understand why everyone couldn't get all the notes in any given chord! She commented that our harmony should be just right—better than her making a face when it wasn't. Roberta was a great gal with a wonderful sense of humor!

Julia Goodfellow CAGO

*Julia Goodfellow is the organist and director of music at Community
Presbyterian Church in Flint, Michigan. She also teaches classes
for parents of challenging children and leads workshops and teacher
in-service trainings on attention deficit disorder.*

Roberta and I had conversed on the phone over a period of a year
before we ever met. It was my responsibility to engage a director for
a United Methodist District Choir Camp in 1974. Having read about
Roberta in *Music Ministry* magazine, I had thought what a great experience it would be for the children to sing under a published composer. Her immediate response was positive. She said she had "done"
choir camps in California. So we continued to communicate via "Ma
Bell" until the camp date finally rolled around.

Roberta arrived while I was busy registering choristers at Crystals
Springs United Methodist Camp. She pulled up in a very small car
which was jam packed.

Being very involved in my job of checking off youngsters and
assigning them to cabins, as well as trying to keep an eye on my own
three young daughters, I forgot for the moment that I was expecting
Roberta. When I saw her get out of the car, I thought to myself,
"That woman has no children with her—she must be lost." But soon
she stepped up to the registration table and announced in her inim-
itable voice, "I'm Roberta Bitgood." And thus began a wonderful
adventure for me.

I was totally amazed at what she was able to accomplish with
those nearly 100 children during the following five days. She had an
incredible ability to focus and to keep them focused. At the very first
rehearsal she got them lined up in order of height and assigned seat-
ing so that when it came time for the concert at the end of the week,
there wouldn't be any question about who went where. Although I
could hardly believe it, in that span of time, the choristers learned at
least a dozen anthems by memory, as well as Horman's cantata "100%
Chance of Rain." It was really inspiring to watch her work.

171

It was some time later, after I had studied with her and been introduced to AGO, that our friendship really deepened. One very foggy night when I had been to Battle Creek for a Guild meeting, I was ready to start back to Jackson, where I lived. I was truly dreading the drive back as the temperature was hovering around freezing and the roads had a glaze of ice on them. Roberta insisted that I stay at her house and drive back in the morning. I gratefully accepted the invitation. Upon arriving at her home, she announced to Bert and her Aunt Marenda, who was visiting from Boston, that they were having a houseguest for the night. Marenda was absolutely aghast, and asked, "Where are you going to put her?" The guest bed where I was to sleep was loaded down with "damn papers" as was the beautiful black dining table. I could really relate to this! With aplomb, Roberta began transferring the piles of things from the bed until, indeed, there was room for me. I knew from that moment on that we were soulmates.

That was the first time I met Bert, and so it was the beginning of my close friendship with him as well. I truly admired the wonderful support he gave Roberta. He was definitely the "great man" behind the "great woman." I couldn't have asked for anyone to be more supportive than they were when, a few years later, I found myself going through a divorce and they became like family. Likewise they were there to rejoice with us when my husband Bill and I were married in 1982, and we spent part of our honeymoon at the cabin at Best View.

Roberta has been a role model in many ways for many people, and I tell her that she continues to be a role model in her acceptance of the infirmities of her senior status. Roberta, among many other things, you will be remembered for your resilience!

Margaret Smith

Margaret Smith, retired from Leila Hospital, is the interim director of North Pointe Woods Retirement Center in Battle Creek. A longtime member of First Congregational Church, she still sings in its choir.

It was apparent the first time I met Roberta that she had almost endless energy. She seemed to attack life with a special vigor. Singing under her direction was always interesting. She could be a hard task-master, but never was unkind. There were times when we were not sure if she was yelling at the tenors or not. We were always short of tenors at that time. I myself sang tenor often; I was one of her so-called "low women." I marveled at her ability to extract any harmonious noises from us all!

I knew she was going to be an interesting person when I saw the canoe on top of her car. It seemed everywhere the car went, the canoe went along. I wondered about it until I had the chance to talk with her and inquired about the canoe. It seemed that she and her husband spent many hours in the canoe on waters both near and far.

We were all aware of her standing in the AGO. Her association with the Guild took her on many distant trips in the U.S. It did not matter that she met herself coming and going! She seemed to have endless energy.

It was fun to watch her play the organ. She was not a very tall person, but watching her play gave you the impression she was of larger stature. I found myself waiting to see if she was going to slide off the bench. Her small feet flew across the foot pedals and her hands did not seem large enough to cover the territory they covered.

We sang songs she wrote and I still recall one concerning eagles' wings. Writing music and scoring pieces were another dimension of Roberta. She was a woman who was not afraid to challenge the status quo, as witnessed by her doctor's degree as well as her serving as the first woman president of the American Guild of Organists. She just seemed to love the challenge.

Joan C. Haggard AAGO

Joan Haggard is organist at First United Methodist Church in Farmington, Michigan. She is a past-dean of the Detroit Chapter of AGO, was chairman for the national AGO convention in Detroit in 1986, and councillor of Region V from 1986 to 1992.

Anyone who has been even remotely associated with Roberta in the past twenty or twenty-five years is well aware of the silver pendant which she always wears on a chain around her neck. The Detroit Chapter of AGO has the honor of being the donor of that pendant.

In 1971, the Detroit Chapter was host to a mid-winter conclave, a regional gathering since discontinued. The logo devised for our conclave materials included the beautifully stylized AGO initials, and a group of organ pipes roughly shaped to resemble an organ-pipe cactus. The chapter was so taken with the AGO symbol that it adopted it for its logo, which is used to this day.

Roberta was a member of Detroit Chapter for a number of years, and brought her unique humor and incredible musical style to the area, as she has done to any area in which she has lived! Even when she had moved to Battle Creek, on the western side of the state, we continued to regard her as one of us. Thus when she became national president of AGO in 1975, we were bursting with joy and pride—the first woman, the first non-New Yorker, the first write-in candidate to be elected!

In 1977, Detroit Chapter was host to the Region V convention. We knew that Roberta would attend and we wanted to honor her in some way that would demonstrate our love for her. The idea developed of creating a pendant in the semblance of the logo. One of the board members knew a silversmith who was able to craft the pendant for us. I had the enormous honor of presenting it to Roberta on the stage of Hill Auditorium in Ann Arbor on "Ann Arbor Day" of our convention. I will never forget her comment as she hefted it—"This is quality stuff!"

It seems only fitting that "quality stuff" should be the symbol of Roberta, who is herself quality stuff!

174

Calvert Shenk FAGO

Calvert Shenk was organist and choirmaster at St. Phillip Catholic Church in Battle Creek when he met Roberta. Since then he has held a church music position in Harrisburg, Virginia, and was the organist and director of music at the Cathedral of St. Paul in Birmingham, Alabama, from 1989 to 2000.

Perhaps my most vivid memory of Roberta Bitgood is of her role in reactivating my participation in the American Guild of Organists. When we were working in churches across the street from each other in Battle Creek, Michigan, in the mid-1970s, I had let my membership lapse. Roberta practically dragged me back into the organization, for which I am forever grateful.

Then she strongly encouraged me to take the Associateship and Fellowship exams, which I passed in successive years. As a friend, a colleague, and most of all, an indefatigable encourager, she made a profound difference in my life and in my professional career.

We frequently attended the same AGO convention, and my wife Ila and I became her shields and buffers at these events after she had assumed the national presidency. From carrying her baggage to getting her out of receptions when she had had enough, we tried to keep her general stress level as low as possible. But however we may have tried to help her, we gained far more in return from her unfailing sense of humor, her shrewd judgment of character, and her strong loyalty and friendship. I have known many celebrated and skilled church musicians in the course of my career but none comes close to being as memorable a personality and as constant a supporter as Roberta Bitgood.

Danford and Emily Byrens

Danford and Emily Byrens had church music positions in Montgomery, Alabama, and then worked as a team in churches in Saginaw and Bay City, Michigan. After Dan retired from his college teaching post in Michigan, they went to the Phillippines in 1990 and taught for four years at Silliman University. They go back periodically, but spend most of their time in Michigan in order to be with their twenty-six grandchildren.

We have two fond memories of Roberta that stand out. In her farewell recital at the Congregational Church in Battle Creek, she played some American music from the late 19th and early 20th centuries. Before the last piece in the group, she apologized for the music in her own amusing way, saying that her friends laugh about this corny music with so many diminished seventh chords. As usual, Roberta was ahead of her time, because now this music is back in fashion and played a lot. After she finished that piece, she played— "by popular demand"—the Bach Toccata and Fugue in D Minor. That whole toccata is based on a diminished seventh chord! It was all I could do to keep from laughing aloud over that circumstance, and the placing of the works on the program one after the other.

Roberta returned a couple of years later to give a program at St. Phillip's Church in Battle Creek for the local chapter of the American Guild of Organists. It was one of the best talks we have ever heard about the Guild and the problems it was facing at the time with several competing factions such as purists and those using electronic instruments—altogether a most delightful speech and evening. But the wonder of it was that as she talked she kept reaching into her large pocket book—actually a kind of over-the-shoulder bag—and fishing out scraps of paper, just exactly the right one for every statistic she wanted. Of course, she could have just pulled out pieces of paper and made up statistics for all we know, but it was a real tour de force. No wonder she guided the Guild so well!

❦

∽ 22 ∾

BEST VIEW

Ronald Arnatt FAGO

Ronald Arnatt is director of music at St. John's Church in Beverly Farms,
Massachusetts, and an editor of ECS Publishing Company of Boston.
He has served as national councillor, vice-president, and president
of the American Guild of Organists.

I was national vice-president of AGO at the time of Roberta's presidency. What made an indelible impression on me was her incredible capacity to recall a wealth of stories to elucidate any point she wanted to make. She had an absolutely extraordinary talent for this.

I also found it most remarkable that she had such an enormous span of musical experience, from the standpoint of repertoire as well as years. I have the utmost admiration for the tremendous contribution she has made to church music.

John Obetz

Dr. John Obetz is a faculty member of the Conservatory of Music at the
University of Missouri at Kansas City, and the current treasurer of the
American Guild of Organists. His national broadcast of The Auditorium
Organ *was heard weekly across the country for more than 25 years.*

There are two areas of association with Roberta that are memorable for me: professional and social. Being a member of the National

Council of the American Guild of Organists during the time Roberta was president afforded me the opportunity to witness her leadership skills, wisdom and patience in dealing with thorny issues, her gracious and generous spirit, and the ability to hold firm to her convictions. She was widely admired and wore the AGO-logo pendant around her neck with much-deserved pride.

Because her daughter and my wife share the same first name, we seem to have a special bond. One evening when we were entertaining the National Council in our home, I remember her thrill at seeing a large wheel of Brie cheese on the table. She loved Brie more than any other cheese, and it made such an impression on her that she reminded me of it many times after.

Roberta's Christmas newsletters were always crammed with activities that filled her busy schedule and were an inspiration for any church musician, let alone those anticipating retirement.

The organ and church-music world will always be indebted to Roberta for her music, her leadership, her gracious spirit, and her undying enthusiasm for our art.

Sue Mitchell-Wallace FAGO

Sue Mitchell-Wallace is a frequent recitalist, clinician, and commissioned composer. She has been Councillor for Education of the American Guild of Organists since 1996.

During my early years as a new member of the American Guild of Organists, Roberta Bitgood was my idol. She was a consummate performer, composer, church musician, teacher, esteemed leader, and most importantly, great supporter of young artists and composers. She readily offered words of encouragement and many opportunities to worthy young musicians. Her sense of humor and extraordinary "people skills" in combination with keen erudition brought her well-deserved renown and meritorious accomplishments.

Some favorite memories include her amazingly humorous rendition of Alfred Hollins's "Trumpet Minuet" and her reminiscences of taking the Fellowship exam at such a young age and learning that she had indeed passed.

At the Denver AGO convention in 1998, it was my privilege to be present at a dinner given in her honor and hosted by her devoted former student Dr. Carl Staplin. Roberta was the life of the party and entertained us all with her wit and wisdom. Thanks be to God for the gift of her life in so many lives.

Brian Rogers

Brian Rogers was college librarian of Connecticut College from 1975 until 1993, and special collections librarian from 1993 until his retirement in 1999.

My first exposure to the church organ had nothing to do with pipes and stops, but with the pedals, that unique feature of the instrument that is both its crowning glory and arguably its greatest challenge. Our church had a Hammond electronic organ, vintage 1940, positioned, like the great theater organs of yesteryear, at the front, and to one side, with the organist's back to the congregation. A ten-year-old sitting in the front row could watch the organist's feet, and I marveled both at the dexterity on display and the sonic result. I was the only person in the front row, of course—in our church, as in most, the members of the congregation occupied the first two or three pews only on Easter, perhaps also at Christmas, when they could not be accommodated in the middle and back rows.

For the rest of the year, only the pedal-watcher—uninhibited by virtue of youth's naivete and emboldened by the fact that my father was the minister—sat up front.

And where is Roberta Bitgood in this memoir? She enters at the point where I first began to comprehend the differences between a pipe organ and an electronic Hammond. Roberta came to Alfred, New York, just up the road from my hometown, as a faculty member and guest artist at the annual Church Music Institute. Directed by the late, indefatigable Lois Boren Scholes, the institutes were held for several years in the forties and fifties, attracting organists and choir directors from around the country for an intensive week of workshops, lectures, organ recitals, and a grand culminating event featuring the attendees assembled as the institute choir. Here, for the first time, I heard choral music performed with authority and confidence, accompanied gloriously with the organ, and it was a revelation.

Those culminating evenings of hymns, anthems, and organ works were as memorable for the participants as for the audience, and were especially so for an impressionable kid just into his teens. The choir's response to the inspired direction of Roberta Bitgood, Robert Fountain, and other nationally known conductor/performers, after a week of sight-reading, study, and rehearsal, was imbued with the unique conviction that only dedicated church musicians could bring to such an occasion. The charismatic personalities of Roberta and the other faculty members, their wit, their utter professionalism from years of experience with the liturgical repertoire (from the anonymous composers of "ancient alleluias" to the newest generation) drew out the very best of the singers.

The organ component of the institutes—half of the week's curriculum, as I recall—was centered on the Rosebush Memorial, a fine 1930s Moller in the Alfred Seventh Day Baptist Church. In one of many memorable recitals the organist, whose name is now lost to me, discussed the Bach prelude and fugue he was about to play and suggested that as the theme of the fugue recurred on its stately, inevitable way it would at last begin to glow, and he cupped his hands as though holding a precious object radiating light from within. The imagery was potent, the sound deeply thrilling.

Those extraordinary services of worship through music linger in the memory, and, as alumni will attest, Roberta Bitgood was a key figure in them. My father served as chaplain for some of the institutes, and I think he once introduced me to Roberta. This would have been like meeting a movie star, for she was one of the guiding lights of the program and that perforce made her a star.

Twenty-five years later we came to New London, Connecticut, where I had been appointed director of the Connecticut College

Library. In prior years my wife and I had sung in church choirs and every now and then we encountered the name of Roberta Bitgood on the sheet music in our hands, or on the back where publishers list other works in print. So it was a pleasant surprise to learn that Roberta Bitgood was not only a graduate of Connecticut College, but lived a scant three miles away and was a frequent visitor to our Greer Music Library. As an active choir director and organist she made good use of the music library's excellent collection of scores and recordings, and saw to it that it had copies of her compositions. Every year at Alumni Reunion she played the Harkness Chapel Austin for the Sunday morning Service of Remembrance, an event treasured by those in attendance for the memorable sense of uplift and consolation provided by Roberta's music.

But Roberta was not seen only in the music library, Harkness Chapel, or the area churches she served until her recent retirement. We know that her music interests have always extended far beyond the organ console and the choir loft. Go to any concert, recital, or evensong in southeastern Connecticut and Roberta is likely to be there. The bond between music lovers strengthens quickly as they compare notes during intermissions, or over post-concert refreshments, and in our first such encounter with Roberta we acknowledged that our lives had intersected years before in a little university town in western New York that had a historic church with a fine pipe organ. The only thing that cements friendship more firmly than the shared love of music is, of course, shared personal history, and we have been proud to be numbered among Roberta's countless friends these past twenty-five years.

When the name of Connecticut College still included the words "for Women," my predecessor in the library had engaged in an effort to acquire letters and other primary research materials relating to outstanding American women, on the order of collections then being formed at Smith and Radcliffe. Our collection eventually included significant holdings on Frances Perkins, the first woman Cabinet member; Belle Moskowitz, a key player in the history of the Democratic Party and adviser to Governor Alfred E. Smith of New

York; Alice Hamilton, one of the first women to attend Harvard Medical School, later a powerful voice warning of the dangers of lead paint and other industrial toxins; Prudence Crandall, the 19th century educator who defied the attitudes of her time by opening a school in Connecticut for young African-American girls; and others. The library's priorities shifted, however, and this collection did not grow for some years until it suddenly occurred to me that the papers of Roberta Bitgood, a local girl who had become one of the college's best known alumni, should be preserved and, like the archival material acquired years before, made available to posterity. I think Roberta was not at first convinced of the value of this, but several visits to her home to examine her files and boxes led eventually to the removal of most of them to the Special Collections department of the Charles E. Shain Library.

Items from the archive provided a rich supply of material for an exhibit I prepared for display in Harkness Chapel during the 1993 Roberta Bitgood Jubilee sponsored by the local American Guild of Organists chapter. The archive is being sorted and arranged by the College's music librarian, Carolyn A. Johnson, herself a church organist and choir director, and a description of it appears at the back of this volume. For many personal and professional reasons I am deeply gratified that a documentary record of Roberta Bitgood's career will be permanently available to any who wish to consult it. The Roberta Bitgood Archive has been listed in recent editions of the Directory of Special Libraries and Information Centers and in due course will be publicized in other printed and Internet-based research tools. Together with her many compositions for choir and organ, the existence of the archive ensures that the achievement of Roberta Bitgood will long serve as an inspiration to church musicians everywhere—indeed, to all who find spiritual joy and renewal in the music of Christian worship.

Alan D. McNeely

Alan McNeely is president of the McNeely Organ Company of Waterford, Connecticut.

My family and I have known Roberta for all of our lives. My Dad was an organist here and grew up with Roberta. As I was growing up in the fifties and sixties, Roberta always came back to her hometown during the summers and often substituted as summer organist at the Groton Congregational Church across the river. My Dad would take "sick" Sundays off from his own church job so that we could attend the Groton service to hear her play. We were not alone. Roberta had quite a number of fans in this area, and the summer Sundays saw many other organ lovers and organists in the congregation—all impatiently waiting for the long-winded minister to finish the sermon so we could all go see and talk with Roberta! I remember those services well. They usually included a Roberta-"arranged" piece or two for the prelude and some big, recital type of composition for the postlude. The fans would gather around the console and whoever was closest would turn the pages for her! She was always most gracious to all of her fans and very interested in anyone who was an organist or an organ student.

In the 1950s, the fashionable Episcopal church in New London was searching for a new organist-choirmaster. The job had always been held by a man and the English rector was determined to continue that tradition. After reviewing the applicants, he consulted with Roberta as to who she felt was the most qualified. To Roberta, there was no question that it should be a lady named Beatrice H. Fisk, who had organized the local AGO chapter a few years earlier. The rector hesitated, as he felt that a woman was not going to do well. Roberta insisted that Beatrice was the *only* person who could play *that* organ in *that* church and the obstinate rector finally crumbled.

Back in the early 1960s, I made the decision to become a pipe organ builder. This met with Roberta's firm approval and she has supported my career over the past thirty or so years. In the late 1960s, we had just finished a small unit organ, and into the church walks Roberta while we were tuning it. She sat down and played the *entire* Vierne Symphony V from memory on it, and then we had a long talk. She was in Battle Creek back then, and had a young friend there who kept the big Congregational organ playing for her. She told many humorous stories about her career out there, and how the organ would mess up right at the wrong times!

I eventually was hired by Austin Organs as a field organ installation technician, and did this mostly full-time from 1972 to 1982. Sometime in the late 1970s, we were installing a large new organ in LaJolla, California, and I remember we were connecting the wires in the back of the console when who should come in to see the new organ but Roberta! She was in town to play a recital at another church and heard about the new organ, so she had driven over to have a look at it.

When Roberta returned to her family home here in Quaker Hill, Connecticut, she began attending the New London County AGO meetings and eventually served as dean. She often spoke fondly of her years as national president of AGO.

She soon became the organist at the Episcopal church in Mystic, Connecticut, playing an awful Estey-Wicks organ to which she managed to have a Moller trumpet added. Around this time, her husband Bert died, and she arranged the music and played for his memorial service at the Episcopal church.

Then she developed knee problems and entered the hospital in New London to have two nylon knee joints installed. I loaned her a portable cassette player with headphones and a bunch of English cathedral organ-choir tapes which kept her occupied during her recovery period. She often called her local friends from the hospital, and one night she called me and asked me to bring her some ice cream. This was not on her recovery diet but "Just who was the doctor to say what she could and could not eat." I bought a tub of vanilla ice cream and took it in to her, which she quickly consumed!

In 1987, our firm built a very large organ for the Navy base chapel in Groton, Connecticut. Roberta stopped in often to watch the progress, especially during the voicing and tonal finishing work. Arrangements were made to have Charles Krigbaum play the dedication recital and Roberta wrote "Toccata on the Navy Hymn," which premiered at this recital. This unique piece involved the audience who stood and sang the first verse of the hymn at the end while the toccata was being played in full force!

Although officially "retired," Roberta was still traveling all over the country playing recitals and weddings for friends and their children, besides doing AGO workshops. It was not uncommon for Dr. John Anthony, the Connecticut College organist, or myself to receive a late night telephone call asking for a ride to the airport in a few days. On one occasion, I drove her to the Hartford airport on a Sunday afternoon. She flew to Buffalo, played for a wedding, and then flew back home that evening when I picked her up and drove her home. She was at least 82 years old at that time!

After her recovery from the knee operation, Roberta continued in her job as organist and choir director of the Waterford Presbyterian Church, which was then meeting at the Connecticut College Chapel. She developed a very distinguished music program and had a wonderful adult choir made up of local singers of all denominations. She then acquired a few organ students and this retirement of hers became a very busy time. She presented many recitals—in fact, going to a Sunday church service at the church where Roberta played was like attending an organ recital interrupted by an "unnecessary" sermon!

In a few years, the growing Presbyterian congregation had enough money saved up to purchase land and design a new church building here in Waterford. Roberta called us early in the planning process. She had demanded that the church get a real pipe organ. This seemed to be financially impossible at the time but to please—and keep— Roberta, they agreed to the idea. The organ was built by our firm, and Roberta and I designed the instrument on her dining room table one evening. The organ was and is a great success, mostly due to her insistence that carpeting be limited in the sanctuary. She had to fight with the building committee to get her way on this issue, but she won.

Not yet busy enough with music, Roberta took the job at the local synagogue, which she really enjoyed.

Here I will include the specification of the Crossroads Presbyterian organ, which will perhaps give you some grasp of Roberta's thoughts on a good design for a small church service instrument:

GREAT
Principal	8
Bourdon	8 (wood)
Gemshorn	8 (enclosed in Swell)
Octave	4
Open Flute	4 (enclosed in Swell)
Fifteenth	2
Mixture III	19, 22, 26
Chimes	
Great	4
Swell to Great	16, 8, 4

SWELL
Chimney Flute	8
Viola	8
Viola Celeste	8
Geigen Principal	4
Nazard	2 2/3
Block Flute	2
Trumpet	8
Swell 16, Unison off,	4
Tremolo	

PEDAL
Subbass	16
Gemshorn	16 (Great ext.)
Octave	8
Bourdon	8
Choral Bass	4
Trumpet	16
Great	8
Swell	8, 4

Electro-pneumatic action, moveable console

This organ is all straight with the exception of the 16-foot Gemshorn and Pedal Trumpet. The Nazard was very important as it allowed a "fake" clarinet sound—a favorite of Roberta's for solo use.

Roberta revived her anthem, "Except the Lord Build the House," for the dedication of the church, and a few weeks later she played the organ dedication recital. The organ has been heard many times at AGO member recitals and, with Roberta playing together with her friend Dr. John Anthony, for "4 hands and 4 feet" organ music!

Roberta's unlimited energy produced an organ recital every Christmas Eve at 11 p.m., and she taught the entire congregation Handel's "Hallelujah" chorus, which they sang every Christmas Eve and Easter.

In 1993, a special jubilee was planned by the local AGO chapter for Roberta's 85th birthday. This was quite an event, with people coming from all over the world to attend the weekend's festivities. Many tributes were made—among them, the singing of Corliss Arnold's "Ode to Roberta," accompanied by AGO members blowing wooden organ pipes!

In 1994, we were building a tracker organ for the front of the local Catholic cathedral. Roberta stopped in at our shop every day for weeks on end to watch the building process from design to the voicing of the pipes. She was fascinated with the mechanics of organs but her real specialty was playing, teaching, and composing.

On Easter Sunday, 1999, Roberta officially retired from her position at Crossroads Presbyterian Church, at age 91. The congregation gave her a special reception, and even today I miss seeing her Honda parked in the church lot when I make my way to our shop each day. Roberta was a very strict practicer, by the way, and usually went to the church for several hours each day to prepare for her Sunday services.

Roberta is truly a great lady who has done much to encourage and promote interest in the organ among young people. She has been a great help to me in my career, especially in helping me understand the real need for, and use of, certain tonal designs and colors in pipe organs. For years, we would have lengthy telephone conversations on Sunday evenings which were instructive and fun for each of us.

Roberta was and is completely dedicated to pipe organs and church and organ music. In fact, she has the largest collection of organ sheet and book music I have ever seen. Not only that, she has been most generous with sharing this music and her ideas about playing it. I believe Roberta felt that the Gospel was better conveyed through organ, instrumental, and choral music than through lengthy, and usually boring, homilies and sermons. I consider her one of my best and closest friends, even though she is some 43 years older than I am. Her encouragement of young musicians throughout her career has been unexcelled.

Michael Noonan

Michael Noonan teaches instrumental music at Wheeler Middle and High Schools in North Stonington, Connecticut, and has played the Estey organ at North Stonington Congregational Church since 1987.

When I was fifteen, I began studying the organ with Roberta and I took to heart her admonition to wear my organ shoes only at the organ. But I was a percussionist as well, and one Sunday I was to play the timpani as well as the organ. When Roberta saw me changing my shoes in the middle of the service, she was so startled that she asked me, "What are you doing?" I gave the only answer possible—that I knew I should wear my organ shoes only at the organ!

I was able to travel with Roberta to turn pages for her whenever she gave recitals, and this gave me exposure to numerous organs. The experience of page turning for those recitals was, of course, nerve wracking but at the same time thrilling!

In 1992, I had the privilege of sharing the dedicatory recital of the newly refurbished organ at St. Mark's Episcopal Church in Mystic, where Roberta and I are still members.

Shirley V. Alderson

*Shirley Alderson was a longtime member of Roberta Bitgood's choir
at Crossroads Presbyterian Church in Waterford, Connecticut.
She is a church deacon and, prior to her retirement,
operated a day care in her home for many years.*

It was in 1984 that Dr. Roberta Bitgood first attended a Sunday service of our church, then named Waterford Presbyterian, which met at Harkness Chapel on the Connecticut College campus in New London.

As I recall, our organist, Norma Branch, realizing that Dr. Bitgood was in the congregation, acknowledged her and her talents during our sharing of Joys and Concerns that Sunday. She concluded by inviting Dr. Bitgood to play the postlude for us, which she did with her special talent and usual aplomb.

Since Norma Branch and her husband were planning an extended trip, we were looking for someone to fill in as organist and choir director on a part-time basis. That someone turned out to be Dr. Bitgood, who quickly became Roberta or "Dr. B" to those of us in the choir. Roberta filled that position ably for 14 years, moving with us when the church, renamed Crossroads Presbyterian, moved to its own building in 1989. She was responsible for the installation of a pipe organ in our church, the first and only one in the town of Waterford.

During Roberta's tenure, our choir grew and participated in many ecumenical services and choir festivals in churches and synagogues on both sides of the Thames River. At one point, she planned and put together a choir festival which included former members of her "Bitgood Kids" choir from Bloomfield College and Seminary, in New Jersey. What a wonderful weekend that was.

We would meet for choir rehearsals at the chapel on Thursday nights from 7 to 9 p.m. One winter, due to the cold weather, cold chapel, and the fact that most of our members lived in the Great Neck area of Waterford, we decided to move our rehearsals to the home of Jim and Ethel Kyle on Great Neck Road. I remember that

Roberta wasn't too happy with this arrangement because there were too many "easy" chairs for people to sit in. Her feeling was that no one could sing well slouched down in an easy chair.

One Sunday in October of 1989, we began our service at Harkness Chapel and, halfway through the service, migrated to our brand new building on Cross Road in Waterford. As I recall, there had been a brief period of tension between the pastor, Rev. Dr. John Webster, and Roberta as to whether or not we should enter the church with or without music. I can't remember just who won out, but no matter, it was a joyous day for all.

At that time, Roberta was also playing the organ on Friday evenings at Temple Emanu-El on Dayton Road. There was one occasion when we participated in a musical service there, singing in Hebrew.

Roberta has generously shared the talent God gave her with the Adult Day Center that meets in our church building during the week. The clients of the Day Center still enjoy her playing. She has also played for our Presbyterian Women's evening meetings—playing "Happy Birthday" during coffee hour more times than she probably wants to remember.

There comes a time in all our lives when the responsibilities of work take on a rather "heavy" feeling, leaving frayed nerves and confusion. This occurred during Roberta's leadership of the choir. Some changes became necessary and they were made. For a short period, Roberta became our accompanist at choir rehearsals and Madelyn Shafer took on the responsibilities of choir director. This arrangement was, I believe, rather painful for Roberta. It was decided after a discussion with Roberta and her daughter, Grace, that she would be our organist only, and she performed gracefully in this capacity for another two years. Subsequently it was discovered that Roberta was suffering from the effects of macular degeneration, and so it was in April of 1999 that she decided to retire for the third time in her life.

In October of 1999, we were blessed to hear Roberta, John Anthony, and Mike Noonan in an organ recital at Crossroads, followed by a reception. The grand finale of the recital was a "stump the organist" free-for-all hymn sing with members of the congregation calling out hymn numbers at random and Roberta playing them. Needless to say, she was never "stumped."

This has been a difficult transition for Roberta and the congregation. There is no one who can replace Roberta—her talent, her unique personality, and her many interesting tales of years past as she cut her niche in what had been pretty much a male profession. We miss her greatly.

During her tenure at Crossroads, I was privileged to have Roberta become one of my very dearest friends. We spent many Thursday evenings at BeeBee's Dairy having supper before choir rehearsal. And Roberta, always the swimmer, was a frequent visitor to our home and pool on Great Neck Road. It was always a pleasure to include her, and her family, in our various family celebrations. She has given me a deeper awareness of the joy of classical music—which I will always associate with her.

Marianna Wilcox

Marianna Wilcox is director of The Anglican Singers, who perform choral evensong at St. James' Episcopal Church in New London and other venues throughout New England.

One of the most endearing Roberta quotes I love to repeat goes something like this— "I've always thought that an organist was not *really* good unless someone in the congregation complained that the organ was too loud!"

E. Ellsworth Watson, Jr.

Ellsworth "Doc" Watson was raised in New London and Quaker Hill, Connecticut, where his family maintained a long-standing friendship with the Bitgood family. Following service as a medic in World War II, he worked as an outside salesman in automotive wares and for Kendall Lubricants until his retirement in 1988. He continues to enjoy trap and skeet shooting once a week at the Rockville Fish and Game Club.

191

The friendship of the Prentis and Dotzauer families began in the late 1890s when Marenda Prentis, Roberta's aunt, was attending Saltonstall Grade School in New London, Connecticut. Mrs. Prentis said to her daughter, "Now Marenda, I want you to meet the Dotzauer family, who live on Coit Street. They are a fine upstanding family and you have permission to go visit them after school, as long as you are home before dark." It was then that Marenda, born in 1894, met my mother, Mabel, born in 1892, the eldest of the four Dotzauer girls. They became lifelong friends.

Roberta came along in 1908. Grace and Robert Bitgood, her parents, lived with the Prentis family until Robert bought the Quaker Hill property and house at Best View.

My mother and father were married in 1914, and I was born in 1915. I never got to know Roberta's parents until after I finished high school. It was then that Roberta's mother told me that, if I was willing to drive her wherever she wished to go, I could have the use of their 1932 Ford Victoria automobile. So, at the age of nineteen, in 1934, I took "possession" of the car. Roberta was away studying for her master's degree and her doctorate in sacred music and composition. It was not until 1940 when we moved to Hartford, Connecticut, that I became acquainted with Roberta and, soon thereafter, two-year-old Grace Claire.

During the time I had the use of the Ford Victoria, I spent many hours driving Grace Bitgood hither and yon. Also, I took Mr. Prentis out for rides. He was in his eighties during those years of the Depression and enjoyed getting out and around.

My family had moved to Quaker Hill, Connecticut, and Best View in 1925, and I had often spent time with Robert Bitgood down on the cove shore, fishing and feeding his large flock of ducks.

I did not get to know Roberta well until she returned to Connecticut to live. Since then, I've been invited to and have attended many of her recitals and concerts here. And for many years, my wife and I have invited Roberta to accompany us to band concerts at the U.S. Coast Guard Academy in New London. She knows many members of the band.

After the members of my family passed away, I, being the only survivor, decided to carry on the closeness our families had enjoyed with Roberta, Bert, and Grace Claire.

If it weren't for the use of the Ford Victoria—a grand car in its day—I would never have known the Prentis and Bitgood family. I was told that the old car, in bad shape, had been sold sometime during the the fifties for one hundred dollars. Now Roberta is in her nineties, and my wife and I are still making trips from South Windsor, Connecticut, to see her. She is the Grand Old Lady of the organ world and we relish the opportunity to visit her.

John Anthony

John Anthony is the college organist and an associate professor of music at Connecticut College, as well as organist and choirmaster at St. John's Episcopal Church in Niantic, Connecticut. Dr. Anthony delivered the following remarks at a luncheon celebration on the occasion of Roberta's 90th birthday, January 15, 1998.

Roberta Bitgood Wiersma—we've been privileged to know her as a composer, a teacher and organist, an AGO member and officer, a faithful alumna of Connecticut College, and a devoted family member and friend. Most of all, we've been fortunate to know Roberta as a rare and wonderful human being.

THE COMPOSER

There have been many Bitgood celebrations over the years.

Here in New London we especially remember the Bitgood Jubilee on the occasion of Roberta's 85th birthday, in 1993. People came from all over the country for concerts, a testimonial dinner and a wonderful display of memorabilia. It was held on the Connecticut College campus.

More recently there was a Bitgood Festival organized by David Spicer in Wethersfield, Connecticut.

This Sunday, Roberta and I and other organists (perhaps some who have not even chosen their music yet!) will perform composi-tions by Roberta in Sunday services.

Roberta's music has been sung and played by many thousands of choristers and organists in the 68–69 years since she first went to New York City.

TEACHER, RECITALIST, ORGANIST

Roberta has taught countless students over the years—and she is still teaching! Some names that come to my mind, because I know them, are Carl Staplin, Michael Noonan, Julie Goodfellow and her present student, Matthew Kelly. She has also worked tirelessly with her friend and student Judy Culler, a talented string player.

Roberta has played recitals everywhere—in small towns and in large cities. About ten years ago I was present to hear her when she played the world-famous organ at Methuen, Massachusetts, on that renowned summer organ series. She practiced like a slave and she played magnificently!

A number of years ago, Alan McNeely built the organ in Rober-ta's present church—Crossroads Presbyterian. As Roberta likes to point out, it is the only pipe organ in Waterford and the only organ in the area with a moveable console—perfect for recitals. Roberta has given numerous recitals there to help raise money to pay for the organ.

In addition to her work as a recitalist, Roberta has served many churches and synagogues across the country. Most of us here remember her devoted service in Greater New London after her so-called retire-ment to Quaker Hill about 1976—St. Mark's Episcopal in Mystic; Crossroads Presbyterian (first at Harkness Chapel and then in their new building); Temple Emanu-El; and her service to Connecticut Col-lege at numerous alumni memorial services during college reunions.

Roberta's primary interest as an organist and a teacher has always been in the *recruitment* of new organists, many as young students—high school and college-age—but many older students as well. Her motto to anyone, young or old, who shows the least interest or curiosity in the organ has been: "Try it—it's fun!" She has proclaimed this for over 70 years—and she is *still* proclaiming it!

AMERICAN GUILD OF ORGANISTS

We might call her Miss, Mrs., or Ms. AGO.

In approximately 65 years, Roberta has probably attended about 650 chapter meetings. She has attended countless national conventions, starting about 1932, and most recently the Centennial National Convention in New York in 1996. She next attended the Berkshire Regional Convention in Massachusetts and will be honored at the upcoming national convention in Denver this summer. Roberta served six years as national president of the AGO, the first woman to be elected to that position. Over the years she also has served as dean of many Guild chapters, including several years as dean of our own local chapter.

I would like to read a number of letters from current national, regional, and local Guild officers: Maggie Kemper, current national president; Vickie Wagner, current Region I councillor; John Anthony, current district convener for Connecticut; and Elma Frysinger, current dean, New London County Chapter

CONNECTICUT COLLEGE ALUMNA

Although Roberta, Class of '28, always likes to remind me that her Aunt Marenda Prentis, Class of '19, and therefore a member of the *first* graduating class, was more "rah-rah" college than she, Roberta has always been a wonderfully faithful and hard-working alum.

Roberta was one of the first, if not the first, student to graduate as an organ major. Roberta later received the Connecticut College Medal—the highest award the College can bestow on an alum for her achievement and dedication to the College. Roberta also served for many years as class agent for the Class of 1928 to raise alumnae gifts for the College.

A FAMILY

As Roberta has pointed out to me on many occasions, she comes from a family of *strong women!* Her grandmother the Suffragette; her mother a devoted church woman who travelled widely to make speeches for missions; and her Aunt Marenda, who received a graduate degree in social work from Yale and went on to Philadelphia, to work in settlement houses, and then to Boston, where she worked until retirement.

Indeed, Roberta was one of the original liberated women. After graduate study in New York City, Roberta played at the Presbyterian Church in Bloomfield, New Jersey, and eventually taught at Bloomfield College, a school that trained Presbyterian ministers. Here this professor, this liberated woman, fell in love with a young seminarian of German heritage with a strangely spelled name—Gijsbert Wiersma. He became, or perhaps already was, simply Bert.

Certainly that is the way I remember him. They were married just before World War II and produced their gift to the next generation—Grace. What a wonderful name! Bert and Roberta clung to each other and supported each other, moving all over the country and into retirement, until his untimely death. Roberta, strong as ever, played the organ for Bert's funeral at St. Mark's in Mystic.

Roberta was a devoted niece to her Aunt Marenda, who died a few years ago at the age of 98. Roberta has done all she could to support her Bitgood relatives, and she has kept in close touch with the many Wiersma in-laws.

But it is to her only child, so aptly named Grace, that we return. Who could have been more proud than Roberta when she travelled to Berkeley, California, to be present when Grace received her Ph.D. in Chinese. I know, because I took her to and picked her up at the Providence airport! Grace and Roberta have grown even closer in recent years, and now they communicate via e-mail.

Several years ago a new person entered what had become the duo of Grace and Roberta, in the form of a beloved son-in-law—Stuart Kiang. I'm not sure Stuart knew what he was getting into! But no one could have been more devoted to Grace and Roberta—and to have fit in so well. Stuart is a man of great intellect, charm, and sensitivity, and most importantly in *this* family—he has a sense of humor!

FRIENDS

Roberta is a woman surrounded by friends. Anyone who has been as active across the country and has held as many diverse positions as she has, is bound to have many friends. Anyone who sends 980 Christmas letters each year is a woman of *friends!*

Roberta, as you know, can go into any group and either find someone she knows already—or perhaps knew 50 years ago, in another life—or find someone she just met last week. All of us here, if we are not relatives, are here as *friends*. Some, like Lilla (Linkletter) Stuart, who was in her first junior choir at the Methodist Church in New London, or like Harriet Hofrichter from Buffalo, Roberta has known for decades. Some she has only met in the past year or two. I consider myself one of Roberta's new friends—I have only known her for 22 years.

Many of you are fellow organists; some are members of her church; some are former students; some are people who have helped Roberta remain independent as she has grown older. You all mean the world to Roberta and your presence here attests to that.

A HUMAN BEING

Finally, Roberta is being honored as a remarkable person—a woman of commitment, love, compassion, and faith. Roberta is always ready to help and encourage students, colleagues, fellow Guild members, and friends. Roberta is still a faithful minister of music, as she has been for almost 75 years, and her own personal religious faith has been an inspiration to all who have had the privilege of working with her and worshiping with her. She is always ready to give and to forgive—she is always open to others' opinions and accepting of other people as they are.

I suppose if we were describing Roberta in Jewish terms, we would call her a real *Mensch*. Somehow it is not quite the same to call her a real "Frau." Perhaps Grace knows an appropriate Chinese word to describe her, but I believe I will just say a great *human being!*

A Toast to Roberta

We who are gathered here and countless others around the country and many abroad salute you, Roberta Bitgood Wiersma—esteemed *composer*; professional, talented and still active *organist*; devoted and still active *teacher*; devoted member, officer, and *national president* of the American Guild of Organists; faithful and enthusiastic *alumna of Connecticut College*; loving *relative* as niece, wife, mother and mother-in-law; faithful and generous *friend* to thousands; and all-around great *human being!*

To Roberta!

ᴄᴖ

ANTIPHONAL

Grace Wiersma

I sit at Roberta's work table, watching her across the room, as we follow what has become her regular Sunday evening routine in recent years: from 9 to 10:30 pm, she listens with serious concentration to the sounds of her favorite pipe organ program, as relayed by the local public radio station. If she is fortunate, one or two of the program offerings will be pieces that she has played often, either in recital or as parts of her Sunday morning service playing. Such pieces she attends to with particular seriousness, perhaps conducting a few bars, or commenting on the performer's registration or phrasing. We exchange comments occasionally, but as a rule keep to our own thoughts while the sounds pour from the equipment. Tonight, I have chosen to stay for the listening ritual—unlike most Sundays when I am homeward bound by sundown after my weekend visit—in order to address the writing of an afterword for this book.

I grew up with the understanding that sharing my mother with the world at large was to be taken as a matter of course, a normal part of our family life, and in fact the one part that made the world go round for her. Although friends and family members, aware of the circumstances, sometimes expressed concern for my outlook as a child and often contributed by generously entertaining me when my mother had other obligations to fulfill, the project of sharing Roberta actually meant much more than learning how to be a self-sufficient child. Rather than freeing her for public life, our job (my father's and mine) was to join her in it. For me this meant being ready to attend as many musical and church events, dressed in suitable clothes, as one person's schedule could accommodate, to interact significantly with her teachers, colleagues, students and choir members, and to perform in various capacities as a singer, instrumentalist, music librarian or hostess. Not that these requirements were stated in so many words, not at least until long after I had become accustomed to the routines of our corporate family enterprise, and had begun to show signs, as a teenager, of going my own way. The remarkable thing to me now is that through this apprenticeship I learned, as a child, to appreciate not only organ music but organists and to take as a first principle the fact that my mother could make things happen at an organ console.

From this vantage point, as we prepare to offer this book of recollections to the public, I realize that what it represents is the public transformation of our family enterprise, and our roles in it, into a more complex and improvisational project. At issue now is not my welfare, but Roberta's, and how best to maintain her grasp of and participation in the multifarious network of personal and collegial contacts that she herself has built up through single-minded devotion to her profession. In examining the contents of this volume what strikes me with particular force is the extent to which the various memoirs recounted here—whether autobiographical or contributed—all join in communicating a single message. Underlying the degree of celebrity that my mother has enjoyed, whether as performer, educator or just plain raconteur, has been a bedrock of musical competence, verbal wit, and personal sensitivity. Although clouded by age, these qualities shine through in her own recollections as well as in those contributed by friends whose lives she touched.

In publishing this book, it remains for me to express our most grateful thanks to Julia Goodfellow for providing the means of executing it. After the need for a written biography became clear, the puzzling question of who would be equal to the task of getting it onto paper had only one answer. Julie was uniquely qualified as Roberta's student and confidant, and she proved more than willing to surmount the personal sacrifices necessary for her to carve out the time to actually do it. My mother and I are much in her debt and will remain so.

I must also express our thanks to the many individuals who have shared in or facilitated the creation of this work. These include, first and foremost, Agnes Armstrong, who kindly granted permission for us to borrow from her published interviews with my mother, which had previously appeared in *The American Organist* and *The New England Organist*. Agnes also kindly lent photographs from her personal collection, which are credited to her as they appear. Anthony Baglivi and other staff members at the American Guild of Organists national headquarters have kindly provided helpful information and other assistance for which we are very grateful. We also would thank Connecticut College Special Collections Librarian Laurie Deredita and Music Librarian Carolyn Johnson for searching in the Roberta Bitgood Archive and lending special materials for reproduction here, especially the Mikado program from Bloomfield College. Special thanks are also due to Grace Post for her interviews with Roberta on the subject of transportation, as memorialized in the chapter entitled "Wheels." And thanks also to Bloomfield College Reference Librarian Mark Jackson for providing important information on the memoir by Professor Harry Taylor. Additionally we want to thank the New London County chapter of the AGO and Dean Susan Jones for permission to borrow from the official history of the chapter authored by Nancy Phillips, and to reproduce several pages from the program of the Roberta Bitgood Jubilee of 1993. Special thanks, too, are due to Florence and Harold Miller for kindly furnishing copies of several prized photographs, including the shot of Roberta with her mixed glee club and junior choir at First Presbyterian Church, New York. For material relating to the family background of my father, J. Gijsbert Wiersma, we are indebted to an unpublished family chronicle entitled "The Wiersma Story," by the late Dorothea Wiersma MacKay. My husband, Stuart Kiang, has generously provided editorial acumen and advice, and Mary Anne and Bill Stewart of The Bayberry Design Company, LLC have ably shown the way with their creative ideas and technical expertise in the course of producing the book. Finally, heartfelt thanks go to every contributor, for recollections that truly convey the message of this book.

September 3, 2000
Best View

201

APPENDIX A

―――✦―――

PUBLISHED WORKS OF ROBERTA BITGOOD

Anthems

GENERAL

A Prayer for Communion. SATB (Remick)
Be Still and Know that I Am God . . . . SATB (Gray)
Except the Lord Build the House . . . . SATB (Flammer)
Give Me a Faith. . . . . SATB (Gray)
God Himself Is With Us. SATB (Gray)
Grant Us Thy Peace (traditional 3-part round) . . . any 3 (Gray)
Great Is God . . . . U & SATB (Sacred Music Press)
Happy the People. . . . . SATB (Sacred Music Press)
Holy Spirit, Hear Us . . . . SS (Westminster Press)
How Excellent Thy Name (Covenanters Tune). . . SA (Flammer)
Let Us Now Praise Famous Ones . . . . SATB (Stone Chapel Press)
Lord, Above All Other Treasures (Bach) . . . . U (Gray)
Lord, Guard and Guide the Men Who Fly . . . . SATB (J. Fischer)
Lord, Guide Our Thoughts. . . . . SA (Choristers Guild)
My Country Is the World. . . . . SATB (Remick)
My Jesus Is My Lasting Joy (Buxtehude)
　　　　　(2 violins opt.) . . . . U (Gray)
New Meanings for Our Age (with handbells). . . . . U & SATB (Flammer)
Now a New Day (Year) Opens . . . . SAB (J. Fischer)
O Lord, Our God, Arise. U & desc. (Broadman)
Praise, Power, Dominion . . . . SATB (Capella Music Co.)
Prayer Is the Soul's Sincere Desire . . . . SSATBB (Gray)
The Greatest of These Is Love . . . . SATB or SSA (Gray)
The Lord's My Shepherd (with flute) . . . . U (Gray)
The Sons of God . . . . TTBB (Sacred Music Press)
They Shall Walk . . . . SATB (Sacred Music Press)
Thy Temple Is Not Made with Hands . . . . SATB (Hope)
We Come with Songs of Gladness . . . . U & desc. (Broadman)

THANKSGIVING OR GENERAL

A Good Thing It Is to Give Thanks . . . . SATB (Galaxy)
A Song of Triumph (Psalm 98) . . . . SA & SATB (Hope)
Lord, May We Follow (ordinations, anniversaries) . SATB (McAfee Music)
Psalm 92 (It Is Good to Give Thanks) . . . . U (Broadman)
The Glory, Lord of Life, Is Thine . . . . SATB (Gray)

ADVENT OR PALM SUNDAY

Hosanna (Moravian arr. from Gregor) . . . . U & SATB (Gray)
My Heart Is Ready, O God (with flute) . . . . U (Broadman)
Prepare the Way, O Zion . . . . U & desc. (Westminster Press)

CHRISTMAS

Alle Gioie Pastors (Shepards Come)
    (flute optional) . . . . SATB (J. Fischer)
Bring a Torch (French) (with flute) . . . . SS (Sacred Music Press)
Christ the Lord Is Born (New Mexico) . . . . SSA or SATB (Galaxy)
Glory to God . . . . U & SATB (Gray)
Once He Came in Blessing
    (Moravian—also general) . . . . SSATB (Kjos)
Rosa Mystica . . . . SATB (Gray)
Sound Over All Waters (also general) . . . . U & desc. (Westminster Press)
Thanks at Christmas . . . . U (Choristers Guild)
That We Might Find Him Still (with flute) . . . . . . U (Choristers Guild)
The Christmas Candle . . . . U or SATB (Gray)
Wise Men, Seeking Jesus (with flute) . . . . U (Sacred Design)

LENT

Christ Went Up Into the Hills Alone . . . . SA or SATB (Westminster Press)

EASTER

Alleluia! Christ Is Risen. U (Broadman)
Joy Dawned Again on Easter Day. . . . . SA & SATB (Gray)
Once There Was a Garden Fair . . . . SS (Westminster Press)
That Eastertide with Joy Was Bright . . . . U (Westminster Press)

MOTHER'S DAY OR GENERAL

Lord of Life and King of Glory (arr. from Ett)
    (opt. Jr. Choir) . . . . SATB (Flammer)

Responses

All Together Joyfully Sing (book) . . . . Choristers Guild
Choral Benedictions. . . . . SATB (Abingdon)
Closing Responses and Amens . . . . SATB (J. Fischer)
Sixteen Amens from the Oratorios. . . . . SATB (Flammer)

Cantatas

Job (30 minutes) . . . . SATB (Gray)
Joseph (30 minutes) . . . . SATB (Gray)
Let There Be Light (20 minutes—Christmas) . . . . SS (Sacred Music Press)

Sacred Solos

Be Still and Know That I Am God . . . . 3 keys (Gray)
Give Me a Faith. . . . . 3 keys (Gray)
The Greatest of These Is Love . . . . 3 keys (Gray)
  (wedding and general—also published as duet for SA or TB)

Organ Solos

At Eventide (arr. from Bach St. Matthew Passion). (Gray)
Awake, Thou Wintry Earth (arr. from Bach) . . . . . organ and brass quartet (Gray)
Chorale Prelude on "Covenanters Tune" . . . . (Flammer)
Chorale Prelude on "God Himself Is With Us" . . . (Gray)
Chorale Prelude on "Jewels". . . . . (Gray)
Chorale Prelude on "O Master Let Me Walk with
       Thee" . . . . (Sacred Music Press)
Chorale Prelude on "Siloam" . . . . (Gray)
Meditations on "Kingsfold" . . . . (Hinshaw Music, Inc.)
Offertories from Afar—7 short pieces based
       on folk melodies . . . . (Flammer)
On an Ancient Alleluia. (Gray)
Postlude on an Old Spanish Hymn (Madrid) . . . . . (Sacred Music Press)
Rejoice, Give Thanks (organ, 4 brass) . . . . (Hope Publ.)

ↄ

Appendix B

The Roberta Bitgood Archive at Connecticut College

Over a period of several months in 1992 and 1993 Roberta Bitgood presented to the library of her alma mater, Connecticut College, an extensive collection of papers documenting her career as organist, composer, and church musician. One of the most absorbing features of the collection is the scrapbooks she meticulously maintained for more than five decades, beginning with her high school and college years. The scrapbooks provide a detailed, chronological survey of Roberta's career into the 1970's. The collection includes copies of her recital programs, printed orders of worship from the churches she served, and hundreds of clippings. Other files contain correspondence and papers relating to her professional activities (including, notably, the presidency of the American Guild of Organists), and to the awards and citations she received from time to time throughout her career.

The most recent material relates to the 1993 Roberta Bitgood Jubilee sponsored by the New London County chapter of the AGO and held at Connecticut College. At that time Special Collections Librarian Brian Rogers, who oversaw the transfer of the Bitgood Archive to the Charles E. Shain Library, prepared a series of nine exhibit panels illustrating highlights from Roberta's career as reflected in a selection of papers and pictures from the Archive. The exhibit was on view at Harkness Chapel during the Jubilee events, and was later displayed at the Crossroads Presbyterian Church in Waterford. The panels are now preserved as part of the Archive.

The Greer Music Library at Connecticut College has collected Roberta Bitgood's published music for many years, and the Archive has supplemented this with additional published music as well as some manuscripts. A uniquely interesting item is the score of Francis Poulenc's organ concerto, autographed by the composer.

The Bitgood Archive is administered by Shain Library's Department of Special Collections, where it may be consulted by appointment. Preliminary sorting was accomplished in 1994–95, and in 1997 Music Librarian Carolyn Johnson began a more detailed examination and sorting of the material that will lead to a permanent arrangement and a set of Finding Aids. When this work is completed the availability of the Roberta Bitgood Archive to the music research community will be announced in appropriate national and regional publications. Connecticut College is pleased to be able to preserve this unique record of the career of one of its most famous alumni, who became known to the graduates of many classes for her playing at the Harkness Chapel Service of Remembrance during the annual reunions of the 1970s and 1980s. Other notable American women represented in Shain Library's special collections include Rachel Carson, Frances Perkins, 19th century educator Prudence Crandall, philosopher/author Susanne K. Langer, and novelist/essayist Blanche McCrary Boyd.

Connecticut College
Music Librarian:

Carolyn A. Johnson
Greer Music Library
Connecticut College
270 Mohegan Avenue
New London CT 06320
Tel: (860) 439-2710
Email: *cajoh@conncoll.edu*

Connecticut College
Special Collections Librarian:

(Mrs.) Laurie Deredita
Charles E. Shain Library
Connecticut College
270 Mohegan Avenue
New London CT 06320
Tel: (860) 439-2654
Email: *lmder@conncoll.edu*

℮

INDEX OF NAMES

A

Ackerman, Dottie 123
Ackerman, William 122
Alderson, Shirley 105, 189
Anderson, Marian 66
Anthony, John 106, 110, 185, 187, 190, 193
Armstrong, Agnes ix, 37, 43, 90, 201
Armstrong, Greta 26, 81, 111
Armstrong, John 25, 60
Arnatt, Ronald 177
Arnold, Corliss 85, 107, 187

B

Baglivi, Anthony 201
Barrett, Ruth Storner 97
Bauer, William 30, 31
Beach, Mrs. H.H.A. 121
Bell, Nell 135
Benham, Arliss 101, 160
Bitgood
    Doane 5
    Grace Prentis 9, 12, 13, 14, 15, 16, 18, 19, 21, 22, 27, 33, 35, 36, 37, 49, 88
    Elmer 18
    Jesse 23
    Robert Treat 13, 14, 16, 17, 18, 21, 22, 23, 24, 27
Bonnett family 135
Boyd, Blanche McCrary 206
Branch, Norma 104, 189
Brownell, Helen 167
Bryan, Jim 3
Byles, Huntington 13
Byrens, Danford 85, 164, 176
Byrens, Emily 164, 176

C

Carl, William C. 24, 35, 37, 38, 39, 41, 42, 43, 44, 45, 46

Carson, Rachel 206
Carter, Ellen 140
Cherry, Lester 125
Christian, Kay 168
Christopher, Michael 121
Clokey, Joseph 135
Coci, Claire 127
Colburn, Daniel N., II 4
Compton, Mary Elizabeth 50, 96
Coyle, Margaret 9
Crabtree, Alan 148
Crandall, Prudence 182, 206
Crawford, Marsha x
Culler, Dave 145, 146
Culler, Judy 144, 194
Culler, Kevin 146
Culler, Kurt 146

D

Daniels, Pete 67
Daniels, Riley 75
Davis, Becky 167
Davis, Ben 167
Davis, Jane 167
Deal, Ralph 87
Deredita, Laurie 201, 206
Derick, Peter 143
Derick, Robert 121, 142
Derick, Winifred 121
DeYoung, Harry 81
Dickinson, Clarence 44, 66, 135
Doane, Willam Howard 5
Dotzauer, Mabel 192

E

Ebersole, Nellie 81
Erb, J. Lawrence 30, 31, 35, 42
Evans, Ann 157, 158
Evans, Barry 164
Evans, David 164
Evans, Rusty 84, 156, 159

F

Fischle, Mildred 96, 130, 132
Fisk, Beatrice H. 183
Fountain, Robert 180
Fox, Virgil 132
Franck, Mary Lou 137, 138
Franck, Robert 137
Frieling, Bob 147
Frieling, Jean 147
Frieling, Peter 147
Frysinger, Elma 195
Fuhrmeister, Anne 106

G

Gall, Janet (Lynes) 134
Gall, Richard 134, 135
Gall, Wm. Purcell 135
Garden, Charlotte 135
Garn, Beryl 161
Gerow, Denton 77, 80
Gerow, Denton 134
Gibson
    Bobbie 128
    Calder II 125
    Calder III 128
    Michael 128
Gibson family 24
Glover, Raymond 96
Goodfellow, Ann x
Goodfellow, Bill x, 172
Goodfellow, Julia ix, 97, 99, 170, 171, 194, 200
Graham, David 87, 166
Graham, Pat 166
Gray, H. W. 89, 90, 131
Gurney, John 135

H

Hadrill, Phil 170
Haggard, Joan C. 174
Hall, Mary Weber 107
Hamilton, Alice 182

Hammond, Helen 170
Hare, Nancy 105
Harry T. Taylor 119
Hartsough, Beverly 137, 138
Hartsough, Harold 137, 138
Hartsough, Mary Lou 137, 138
Hartsough, Ruth Jones 137
Hedden, Warren 41, 42
Hehr, Clifford N. 76, 129
Heller, Stephen 104, 105
Hill, Jim 85
Hofrichter, Charles 72
Hofrichter, Harriet 197
Holler, John 89
Hoopengardner, Adrian x
Hoopengardner, Martha x
Hoopengardner, Wilda x
Hurlbut, Leola 140
Hurley, Cliff 135

I

Isaac, Fran Delmerico 162

J

Jackson, Mark 201
Jenkins, Frederick 55
Jenkins, Mary Elizabeth 50, 96
Johnson, Carolyn A. 182, 201, 206
Jones, Joyce 106
Jones, Susan 201

K

Kaltrider, William D. 153
Kelly, Brian 69
Kelly, Matthew 194
Kemper, Margaret M. 107, 195
Kiang, Stuart x, 69, 70, 71, 147, 196, 201
Krigbaum, Charles 185
Kuiper, Margaret 164
Kyle, Ethel 189
Kyle, Jim 189

L

Langer, Susanne K. 206
Lau, Dorothy Len 69, 70
Lee, Janet A. 148
Leighton, Phyllis 140
Lincke, Clara Margarete 59
Lincke, Lydia 59
Linkletter, Lilla 197
Loew, Ralph 72, 73, 129
Lynes, Janet 134

M

MacKay, Dorothea Wiersma 201
Manni, Esther 169
Mason, Marilyn 85
McCall, Reginald 39
McCarthy, John 110
McCord, Lillian Mecherle 49, 58
McGinnis, Patrick 16
McNeely, Alan vii, 103, 104, 183, 194
Mealy, Margaret 123
Mecherle, Lillian 49
Mezoff, Carl 151
Miller, Clara Pankow 106, 124
Miller, Florence 201
Miller, Harold 201
Mitchell-Wallace, Sue 178
Moller, Ted 75, 76
Moment, John 135
Moore, Douglas 49
Moskowitz, Belle 181
Moulton, Beverly 137, 138

N

Noonan, Michael 98, 103, 188, 190, 194
Norman, Victor 111
Nykamp, Jean 85, 149

O

Obetz, John 177

P

Pace, Colleen x
Pearson, Helge 78
Pease, Rhenda 165
Perez, Marcus 109
Perkins, Frances 181, 206
Pew, David 63
Phillips, Nancy 3, 201
Pierce, Howard 7, 30
Pierce, Pauline 58
Poister, Arthur 130
Poling, Charles 45, 46, 47, 50
Poling, Daniel 45
Post, Grace 201
Prentis
    Carrie Mason 15, 18, 19, 20, 23, 33, 195
    Grace Robinson 13, 15, 196
    Marenda Elliott 12, 13, 15, 18, 19, 25, 26, 28, 35, 36, 42, 62, 111, 172, 192, 195, 196
    Stephen Avery 15, 18, 19, 23
Preston, Brownie 140
Preston, Jerry 140

R

Reid, Wilda Hoopengardner x
Ritchie, Andrew 141, 142
Ritchie, Shelley 82, 141
Robinson, Clarence 62
Rogers, Brian 179, 205
Rookus, Melvin 155
Root, Herbert 13
Roth, Carl 56
Roubaud, Julie B. 122
Ryder, William 121

S

Sabourin, Bob 85
Scholes, Lois Boren 179
Schuster, Hugh 151
Schweitzer, Albert 6
Shafer, Madelyn 105, 190
Shenk, Calvert 86, 175

Sly, David 160, 168
Smiley, Raymond 50
Smith, Margaret 173
Speiran, Laura x
Spelman, Leslie 98, 99
Spicer, David 193
Stafford, Alisa x
Staplin, Carl B. 96, 97, 107, 130, 132, 179, 194
Staplin, Phyllis 131
Stewart, Mary Anne and Bill x, 201
Stuart, Lilla 197
Swann, Frederick 70

T

Tallenger, Gary 163
Taylor, Harry 201
Taylor, Judy 167
Taylor, Nelda 85, 150, 159
Thomerson, Kathleen 131

U

Ulrich, John 135, 136
Ulrich, Vera 136
Unger, Margaret 159

V

Van Dissel, Kurt 91, 111
Vigeland, Hans 96

W

Wagner, Vickie 195
Watson, E. Ellsworth, Jr. 191

Webster, John C.B. vii, 104, 190
Wells, Mary 58
Wesley, John 18
Westra, Dorothy 121
Westra, Winifred 121
Wheeler, Andy Crocker 71
Wheeler, Donald 122
White, Carol 134, 135
White, Michael M. 135, 139
Wiersma
   Clara Lincke 59
   Dorothea 51, 59, 60, 201
   Grace ix, x, 5, 23, 24, 26, 62, 64, 65, 66, 67, 68, 69, 70, 71, 73, 77, 78, 80, 81, 85, 91, 96, 102, 104, 105, 109, 110, 121, 122, 124, 126, 130, 131, 132, 134, 138, 140, 143, 147, 157, 190, 192, 193, 196, 197, 199
   Greta (Margarete) 26, 60, 81, 111
   Jacob Gijsbert (Bert) 24, 25, 34, 57, 59, 60, 61, 62, 63, 64, 65, 66, 67, 68, 69, 70, 77, 78, 80, 81, 82, 84, 86, 90, 97, 98, 102, 103, 104, 111, 124, 126, 130, 132, 134, 136, 140, 141, 145, 146, 147, 151, 154, 156, 157, 158, 161, 162, 172, 184, 193, 196, 199, 201
   Jacob Tjisse 57, 59
   Tjisse Olfert 59
Wilcox, Marianna 107, 191
Williams, David McK. 38, 44, 89, 90
Williams, Margaret 123
Wood, Dale 97, 141
Wymer, Alice 140
Wymer, Dale 141